Richard Rive
Buckingham Palace, District Six

D1727717

Cornelsen

Richard Rive **Buckingham Palace, District Six**

Herausgegeben von:
Dr. Albert-Reiner Glaap

Verlagsredaktion:
Neil Porter

Gestaltung & technische Umsetzung:
Anna Bakalovič und Annika Preyhs, Berlin

Umschlagillustrationen:
Großes Bild: © Corel Library
Kleines Bild: Cloethe Breytenbach, © Ethnic Art

Herausgeber der Cornelsen Senior English Library:
Prof. Dr. Albert-Reiner Glaap

First published in 1986 by David Philip Publishers,
an imprint of New Africa Books (PTY) Ltd, Cape Town
© 1986 Richard Rive

www.cornelsen.de

1. Auflage, 1. Druck 2006

Alle Drucke dieser Auflage sind inhaltlich unverändert
und können im Unterricht nebeneinander verwendet werden.

© 2006 Cornelsen Verlag, Berlin

Druck: CS-Druck CornelsenStürtz, Berlin

ISBN-13: 978-3-06-031119-4
ISBN-10:   3-06-031119-6

 Inhalt gedruckt auf säurefreiem Papier aus nachhaltiger Forstwirtschaft.

Contents

Abbreviations and Annotations

adj	adjective		**jdm./jdn.**	jemandem/en
adv	adverb		**n**	noun
cf.	confer; see		**p., pp.**	page, pages
derog	derogatory		**pl**	plural
e.g.	exempli gratia; for example		**sb.**	somebody
esp.	especially		**SAE**	South African English
etc.	et cetera; and so on		**sl**	slang
fml	formal		**sth.**	something
i.e.	id est; in other words		**usu.**	usually
infml	informal		**v**	verb

The annotations are arranged chronologically; the first time a word is used is where you will find it explained.

For help about reading and presenting literature in the classroom, cf. **www.learnetix.de/bookshelf**.

Part One:

Morning 1955

Mary

The Abrahams (Malayan Moslems)
Mona
Jungle boys

"Zoot" (Milton September)

I remember

those who used to live in District Six, those who lived in Caledon Street
and Clifton Hill and busy Hanover Street. There are those of us who still
remember the ripe, warm days. Some of us still romanticise and regret when
5 our eyes travel beyond the dead bricks and split treestumps and wind-tossed
sand.

When I was a boy and chirruping ten, a decade after the end of the Second
World War, when I was Tarzan and Batman and could sing 'Rainbow on the
River' like Bobby Breen – in those red-white-and-blue days I remember
10 especially the weekends, which began with the bustle of Friday evenings when
the women came home early from the factories and the men came home late
although they had been paid off early – and the feeling of well-being and
plenty in our house on the upper left-hand side of Caledon Street near St
Mark's Church. We lived in the fourth in a row of five mouldy cottages called
15 'Buckingham Palace' by the locals. The first, 201, the one fartherest from the
church as if by design, was a bluepainted House of Pleasure called the 'Casbah'.
In it lived Mary and The Girls. Next to them at 203, painted bright pink, was
'Winsor Park' (spelt like that), which was occupied by Zoot and The Boys.
Then came 205, the cottage of The Jungles, then ours, then at 209 that of Last-
20 Knight the barber, his wife and three daughters. A sprawling open field
overgrown with weeds and rusty tin cans separated Buckingham Palace from
the church.

Friday evenings were warm and relaxed.

---

4 **regret** (v): Wehmut empfinden   5 **brick**: Backstein   **wind-tossed**: blown by the
wind   7 **chirrupping ten**: (here) be a lively ten-year old   9 **Bobby Breen** (born
1927): Canadian child actor and singer   **red-white-and-blue days**: the time when
South Africa was part of the British Empire (the colours are those of the Union
Jack, the British flag)   10 **bustle**: busy and noisy activity   13 **plenty**: having
enough to live well   14 **mouldy**: shabby, run-down   16 **as if by design**: as if so
planned   20 **barber** (old-fashioned): hairdresser   **sprawl**: stretch
21 **overgrown with weeds**: von Unkraut überwuchert

We felt mellow because it was the week-end and payday. While my sister got dressed to go to the Star or National Bioscope with her boyfriend, since there was no time for her to cook I was sent to Millard's Fish and Chips shop beyond Tennant Street to get the evening's supper. I raced with the south-easter and then forced my way into the shop crowded with customers, the air thick 5
with the smell of stale sawdust, boiling fish oil and sweaty bodies as steam rose from the frying-pans. When I had wriggled my way through the forest of grown-up legs and torsos, I found myself jammed against the counter, always just too late to order from the last batch of fish and chips, and then had to wait, fighting to prevent the breath from being squeezed out of my body, until 10
the next batch of gleaming stockfish and thick fingers of potato chips were hoisted, dripping oil, and spewed out onto the warmers. On the way home I raced to keep the parcels hot, but not so fast that I could not pierce a small hole in the packet and remove a few chips. But this was finally detected by my hawkeyed mother, who knew what was happening in spite of my denials. 15
Saturdays and Sundays were different.
Saturday mornings were brisk, for some men must work and all women must shop. And Hanover Street was crowded and the bazaars and fish-market did a roaring trade. There were groceries to buy on the book and clothes on hire-purchase. 20

Katzen, who was the landlord of Buckingham Palace, had his emporium on the corner of Hanover and Tennant Streets. His shop windows were cluttered with bric-à-brac such as celluloid dolls, huge glass tankards still celebrating the Coronation, rolls of crêpe-de-chine, gramophones and framed and mounted prints of a violently pink-faced King George VI and Queen 25
Elizabeth. After his premises had been broken into six times in so many weeks, Katzen displayed a notice outside his shop, 'Although Katzen has been burgled again, Katzen will never burgle you!' We all knew that there was no chance of the small, Jewish shopkeeper with his walrus moustache and large feet ever climbing through our back windows to steal our radios, but we also felt that he 30
could rob us in other ways. The thieves always seemed to steal his gramophones and crêpe-de-chine and patriotically left the prints of King George VI and his queen.

Saturday mornings Tennant Street, Hanover Street and Castle Bridge heaved and bustled with housewives, peddlers, skollies, urchins, pimps and 35
everybody else. Everybody bought everything on lay-bye and it was all written down in exercise books; Moodley, the Indian general dealer in Caledon Street,

scribbled it on the back of brown paper-bags which he lost when he absent-
mindedly used them as containers for sugarbeans or rice. Everyone also knew
40 *they would have to pay in the end, even those who owed Moodley, although*
when that end was, was extremely flexible and it could be next week or next
year or next never.

Near Seven Steps Mr Angelo Baptiste owned a dark Italian shop from the
ceiling of which hung strings of garlic. His shop also smelt of macaroni and
45 *olive oil. We would tease him in order to hear him swearing volubly in his*
native language.

On Saturday afternoons I went to Star Bioscope with Estelle, Manne and
Broertjie to see that week's exciting episode of 'Zorro Rides Again' in black and
white. We could not stand in any queue to get in because the idea of queues
50 *had not yet reached District Six. So we pushed and tugged and sweated to slip*
through the narrow opening in the iron gates which would allow us into the
foyer where we could purchase the tickets. Estelle, who never feared anyone,   ~Estelle~
simply climbed onto the nearest pair of shoulders at the back of the heaving   ~✓~
mass and then crawled over heads. Once through the gates, we bought our
55 *tickets to sit on the hard seats downstairs, where ushers in soiled, prison-*
warder khaki, shouted loudly and forced us to share seats with whomever they
shoved down beside us. If you raised any objections you were meanly clouted.
(One sadistic usher took to riding up and down the aisle on a bicycle, lashing

---

1 **mellow**: relaxed and happy   2 **bioscope** (SAE): cinema   4 **south-easte**r: wind
that comes from the Indian Ocean   6 **stale sawdust**: vermodertes Sägemehl
7 **wriggle**: move like a snake   8 **torso**: upper part of the body   **jammed**: squashed,
not able to move   12 **hoist sth.**: lift sth.   **spew sth. out**: etwas ausspeien
15 **hawkeyed**: sharp-eyed   17 **brisk**: busy   19 **do a roaring trade**: do good
business   19 **buy on the book** (old-fashioned): buy things on credit   23 **cluttered
with sth.**: filled with sth. in a messy way   **bric-à-brac** (sing): small cheap
ornaments   **celluloid**: type of plastic   **tankard**: Krug   24 **the Coronation**: die
Krönung   24–25 **framed and mounted**: gerahmt und aufgezogen   35 **heave and
bustle**: be crowded and busy   **peddler**: street seller   **skolly** (SAE): hooligan, gang
member   **urchin** ['əːtʃɪn]: badly behaved boy   **pimp**: Zuhälter   36 **on lay-bye**:
on credit   38–39 **absent-mindedly**: careless because you are thinking of sth.
else   45 **tease sb.**: provoke sb. with words   **voluble**: loud and noisy   50 **tug**: pull
53–54 **heaving mass**: Gedränge   55 **usher**: cinema attendant   **soiled**: dirty
55–56 **prison-warder**: prison guard   57 **raise objections**: protest   **clout meanly**:
hit unfairly   58 **aisle** [aɪl]: space between rows of seats   **lash out**: hit out

out with his belt at any unfortunate urchin who provoked his displeasure.)
When Estelle, resplendent in his cowboy shirt, three-quarter pants and high-
heeled boots arrived late and stood in the lighted entrance, he would cup his
hands to his mouth and blow a loud strident whistle which only he could blow.
It rose above the packed and heaving auditorium to Manne, who sat in the   5
farthermost corner tight between his girl and the one he was keeping for
Estelle. Manne, heeding the whistle of his leader, would throw lighted matches
into the air, regardless of anyone on whom it landed, like a ship sending up
distress flares. And then Estelle would wade over seats and frightened urchins
in a straight line to his minion and the girl reserved for him.   10

We sat goggle-eyed in the thick, cigarette-smoke dark, watching Zorro
carve out Z's with his whip on the foreheads of those crooks stupid enough to
challenge his dexterity with inferior weapons like six-guns. We munched our
way through half-loaves of split-open brown bread that had whole pieces of
fried fish placed in between. Estelle, who was a successful pickpocket, always   15
paid for the refreshments. When they played the movie of Hamlet, Estelle
whistled and shouted derisively that it was a lot of balls, and Alfie, who was in
Junior Certificate at Trafalgar High and a budding critic, said the outjie spoke
far too much and who ever saw a ghost that looked like that.

And in the evenings we would stand in hushed doorways and tell stories   20
about the legendary figures of District Six, Zoot, Pretty-Boy and Mary, or
show off about our prowess with the local girls, of just talk about the ways of
white folks and how Cissie Gool was fighting for us and showing the white
people a thing or two. And how wonderful it was to live in America and talk
like Charles Starrett and sing like Gene Autry. The young men went to parties   25
or bioscope, and the older men played dominoes and klawerjas on the stoeps,
holding the huge boards between them on their laps, and when they banged
down the dominoes or the cards, hordes of flies would spin up and then settle
down again. The young girls waited for the men to fetch them, all coy, demure
and made up in the latest fashions. The older housewives came out with their   30
wooden benches and sat apart from the men on the stoep and gossiped the
mild evening away.

And the apricot warmth of a summer Sunday morning when almost
everyone slept late and mouldy cocks kept in postage-stamp, asphalt yards
crowed their confined calls to wake no-one in particular. Then the sun rose   35
over-ripe although it was barely six o'clock and the whole District was snoring
and blowing away the fumes of Saturday evening. The gaiety and sheer

abandonment of the previous night had given way to the exhausted sleep of
Sunday morning.

40   I would be sent to buy koeksisters for breakfast at a house next to Bernstein's
Bottle Store, where three unmarried Muslim sisters lived. Their house always
smelt of aniseed and rose water. I would stand in the dark passage awaiting
my turn, watching them fry the light dough until it was golden brown, then dip
it hot and sugary into coconut. They had taken a liking to me and always gave
45 me an extra one wrapped separately which I ate on the way back.

      When the first people had woken from their smoke-filled sleep, the more
righteous washed themselves in zinc tubs in their yards or kitchens (with the
curtains drawn), then put on their Sunday best and searched for hymnbooks
and bibles neglected during the rest of the week. They put on tight patent-
50 leather shoes, had a hurried breakfast of hot coffee and koeksisters, and
walked wincingly up Caledon Street to attend the morning service at St Mark's.
Those less virtuous tossed dreamlessly, fading out the monotony of the week
before at the same job in the same factory for the same wages which were
never enough for groceries and rent and a bit of booze and maybe an evening
55 with the girls at Mary's.

      At midday we were served with the heaviest meal of the week. We sat
around the dining-room table stiff and uncomfortable in our navy-blue best.
After a long drawn-out grace we started with curry and yellow rice rich with

---

2 **resplendent**: looking splendid   7 **heed sth.**: obey sth.   10 **minion**: Schützling,
Untergebener   11 **goggle-eyed**: with eyes wide open; staring   13 **dexterity**:
Geschicklichkeit   **munch sth.**: eat sth. noisily   17 **derisive**: verächtlich   **a lot of
balls** (sl): total nonsense   18 **budding**: angehend   **outjie** (SAE): fellow
20 **hushed**: quiet   22 **show off**: angeben   **prowess** ['praʊɪs]: manly qualities
23 **Cissy Gool**: Coloured lawyer who fought against racism   25 **Charles Starrett,
Gene Autry**: US film stars of westerns   26 **klawerjas**: South African card game
stoep (SAE): veranda; raised area in front of a house   29 **coy**: pretending to be
shy   **demure** [dɪ'mjuə]: shy and very well-behaved   34 **mouldy**: old and ugly
postage-stamp: (here) very small   35 **confined**: gefangen; beengt   37 **gaiety**: fun
37-38 **sheer abandonment**: pure Ausgelassenheit   40 **koeksister** (SAE): type of
doughnut   43 **dough** [dəʊ]: Teig   47 **righteous** ['raɪtʃəs] (n): Rechtschaffende(r)
zinc tub: metal bathtub   49-50 **patent-leather**: Lackleder   51 **wince**: have a
painful expression on your face   52 **toss**: roll from side to side   **fade sth. out**:
make sth. become less clear   54 **booze** [bu:z] (sing; infml): alcoholic drinks
58 **grace**: prayer said before a meal

12

raisins and cinnamon. The curry was pale and anaemic because my aunt, who always lunched with us on Sundays, claimed to suffer from acid winds. But after that we had thick slices of roast and potatoes smothered in gravy, and red beetroot salad. And finally jelly and custard and sometimes bread or rice pudding. 5

In the afternoon, when the adults were snoring heavily, we children would roam the streets, always careful not to soil our Sunday suits. On rare occasions we ventured downtown to the Museum to see the models of Bushmen with big bums or furtively glance at the nude statues in the Art Galleries. What a wicked and enjoyable place the world was. What goings-on. And then we 10 walked back through the Botanical Gardens whooping and shouting and raising havoc deliberately to frighten fragile little white ladies sitting on quiet benches, who would then complain to the attendants about those rude slum children.

Back home the darkness descended from Table Mountain and the 15 streetlamps flickered to life at the tops of their stalks, leaving pools of light at their bases in which we played our games till called inside because it was school tomorrow. It was always school tomorrow on Sunday evenings when we were enjoying ourselves, even when we knew it was vacation time. The hush crept over the District as one by one the lights were switched off or paraffin 20 lamps blown out until there was only the basin of darkness at the foot of the mountain illumined by rows of lamp-post stalks. The streets would empty until in the small hours there were only stray dogs, prowling cats, solitary drunks and hawkers' carts leaning awkwardly with their long shafts against the walls. 25

And I still clearly remember the characters and the incidents.

Mary

In her days of innocence before her personal fall, Mary Bruintjies lived in her own particular Eden, which was a mission station deep in the hearts of the Boland. She was young and buxom and known in those
30 days as Baby-face Mary because of her childlike look of artlessness. She was the only daughter of Pastor Adam Bruintjies. During the day she attended the village primary school where she learnt reading and writing, and at night, when she wasn't at Brigade meetings and was playing instead with the boys on the *werf*, she learnt other things which
35 interested her more. Mary had joined the Church Brigade at first to improve her alibis but, such was her dexterity with the baton, that she was soon promoted to drum major over four young bucks who had challenged her for the position. It was the first time in its history that the Brigade had a girl marching at its head doing tricks to dazzle the eye and
40 excite every male onlooker. And when they marched to church on Sunday mornings in full regalia, her father would watch their arrival proudly from the main door.

Her fall was sudden but not entirely unexpected, especially by those in the know. She was caught one Sunday after church parade with the
45 bass-drummer behind a hayrick. What made matters worse was that the bass-drummer was married and he was caught by his wife, who became suspicious when she saw the bass-drum at home without her husband. Both the guilty parties were still in or at least partially out of uniform. The bass-drummer was forced by his wife to leave the Brigade for health

---

2 **acid winds**: Sodbrennen   3 **smothered in gravy**: in Bratensoße getränkt
4 **beetroot**: Rote Beete   **jelly**: Wackelpudding   **custard**: vanilla-flavoured sauce
7 **roam the streets**: wander around   9 **bum** (infml): Hintern   **furtive**: verstohlen
10 **wicked**: bad, evil   11 **whoop**: make a loud joyful cry   12 **havoc**: chaos
deliberate: intentional   23 **stray dog**: dog without a home   **prowl**: herumstreifen
solitary: on your own   24 **hawker**: Hausierer   29 **buxom**: vollbusig
29 **Boland**: farming area to the north-east of Cape Town   35 **Church Brigade**:
youth movement of the Methodist Church   36 **baton** ['bætɒn]: Tambourstab
37 **buck** (old-fashioned): young man   39 **dazzle sth.**: impress sth.   41 **regalia**:
festive uniform   45 **hayrick**: heap of hay

reasons and Mary was packed off to Cape Town to continue her formal education in the big city.

This was a grave error of judgement on the part of Pastor Adam Bruintjies. He sent his daughter to stay with his maiden sister in Caledon Street, but the sister was too preoccupied with church affairs to bother about her refractory and unrepentant niece. Mary's formal education progressed slowly once she went to high school but her informal education moved forward apace. She retained an interest in uniforms and joined the local Church Brigade, which was bigger, more splendid and belonged to a more established denomination. Her dexterity with the baton was again such that she was soon marching at the head of far more illustrious and glorious columns than the little mission could ever provide. But she could not confine herself to marching and twirling. This time it was the chief bugler whose wife forced him to resign for health reasons. Mary was also asked to leave the Brigade.

At school her teacher's health and reputation declined suddenly after he had helped her a few times privately with her reading. His wife forced him to give up teaching after-hours, and spoke about it to the principal's wife, who also started worrying about her husband's physical condition. Mary's aunt decided that her niece's formal education should come to an end. After a tremendous row Mary left her aunt's home, got a job in a clothing factory, and as Mary Brown (which sounded better than Mary Bruintjies) moved in with the Knights at 209 Caledon Street, the last house in the row nearest the church.

Mr Joseph Knight, his wife and their three daughters lived in somewhat cramped conditions. His unmarried brother Henry, who was two years older than Joseph, boarded with them. Both were slight, nervous men, with such dark complexions that Joseph was known throughout the District as Last-Knight, and his older brother as Knight-Before-Last. Joseph and his brother ran a barber's shop in Tennant Street, and Joseph was chief churchwarden at St Mark's. His wife revelled in his business position and high ecclesiastical office. With seven persons living in a small cottage, life was a bit crowded and Mary and Knight-Before-Last used to go for long walks up the slopes of Devil's Peak to ease the congestion.

After being caught more than once in compromising positions, on one occasion in the chair of the barber's shop after hours, they decided

to get married and hired 201 Caledon Street from Katzen the landlord
when it fell vacant. After his initial enthusiasm for his wife had waned
40 and his amazement at her energy had subsided, Knight-Before-Last
began to fear for his health. One day, at the very end of his tether he
simply took his clothes and ran away and was not seen again in the
District for years. Last-Knight went to search for his brother at 201 and,
when he came home only the following morning, worn out and happy,
45 his wife accused him of lechery and incest and he was forbidden ever to
go back there again.

Although Mary reverted to her former name of Mary Brown, everyone
in the District referred to her simply as Mary. There was only one Mary
and that was the Madam of the Casbah. She was now on her own but
50 not for long. Soon The Girls started moving in. First came The Butterfly
with tattoos on her arms and legs, seeking sanctuary from her common-
law husband who used to beat her. Then came Fiela Vreters whose father
had thrown her out because, as she claimed, he had accused her of
eating too much. True, he was suspicious when her stomach began
55 swelling but this coincided with almost complete loss of appetite. She
went to Mary, who soon got her well again. She just stayed on. Then
came Moena Mooies who had lived with The Jungles at 205 and who
also stayed on after they beat up her white boyfriend. Mary was now in
business. She bought extra beds from Katzen, who generously threw in
60 two framed and mounted prints of King George VI and his queen. Mary
and The Butterfly polished and scrubbed the house, and Moena Mooies
fried koeksisters and samoosas for the potential customers when they

5 **preoccupied**: busy   6 **refractory**: störrisch   **unrepentant**: seeing no reason to
feel sorry   8 **apace**: rapidly   10 **denomination**: Konfession   13 **confine sb. to
sth.**: limit sb. to sth.   **twirl**: twist (sth.) round and round   14 **bugler** [ˈbjuːɡlə]:
person who plays a bugle (= Horn)   21 **tremendous row** [raʊ]: very big and loud
disagreement   24 **row** [rəʊ]: line   26 **cramped**: beengt   27 **board with sb.**: live
with sb. (and pay them rent)   28 **complexion**: skin colour   31 **churchwarden**:
head of church community   **revel in sth.** [ˈrevl]: enjoy sth. very much   35 **ease
the congestion**: (here) give those at home more space   39 **fall vacant** [ˈveɪkənt]:
become empty   **initial**: first   **wane**: become smaller/less   40 **subside**: become less
41 **be at the end of your tether**: vollkommen fertig/am Ende sein   45 **lechery**:
sexual lust   47 **revert to sth.**: go back to sth.   51 **sanctuary**: place of safety

were resting afterwards. At Mary's insistence Katzen had painted the outside of the cottage bright blue (he had lots of blue and pink paint left over) and The Butterfly carefully printed the name Casbah on the wall next to the front door. The house was anything but a fortress. A warm, red, welcoming light was fitted over the entrance, and the cottage was 5 officially opened for business.

Mr Zoot September was employed as handyman and general repairman-cum-bouncer. He was on call in case there were problems with which Mary could not cope, and slept in the backroom. Later he and The Boys lived in the cottage next door. The Jungles at 205 ignored 10 Moena Mooies and barely recognised Mary because she had taken their cousin in. She was called Moena Mooies to distinguish her from their sister and her cousin, also Moena, who was unkindly nicknamed Moena Lelik. The latter had no alternative but to remain virtuous and stay at home. Last-Knight cast interested looks at 201 but was allowed nowhere 15 near until later when there was peace between his wife and Mary. Even then Mrs Knight kept tight control over her churchwarden husband. But when feeling ran high between the two cottages his wife looked in the opposite direction when they drove past in their rickety Studebaker and Last-Knight was forced to concentrate on the road. 20

Mary still practised twirling her baton for old times' sake and on occasions she was persuaded to do so on her front stoep to attract potential customers. The Girls and many of the neighbours gathered around to admire her dexterity. Another thing she retained from her childhood and Brigade days was her membership of the church. She still 25 attended regularly once a month and took communion in spite of the dirty looks she received from the churchwarden's wife. She also paid her church dues promptly on time.

Zoot

Zoot September started life as Milton September. His first name, like
30 those of his brothers Byron and Keats, was given to him by an enthusiastic
aunt who had studied poetry at Zonnebloem for her Primary Lower
Teachers Certificate and had never recovered from the experience.
Milton soon developed a penchant for trouble, from the very first day he
attended school at Zonnebloem, where his maiden aunt taught. He
35 became so excited when he first saw the principal that he peed in his
shorts right there in front of the great man himself. When the principal
scolded him and his aunt clouted him for this, they set permanently in
motion his absolute dislike and disregard for authority and officialdom.
By the time he had passed Standard Five he had run away from four
40 schools.

Milton was the youngest of the five boys who lived with their
widowed mother in Starling Street Flats. Once he had settled down at
the fifth school, again Zonnebloem, because he fell in love with his
teacher he proved to be an avid reader and could write startling although
45 somewhat unorthodox compositions. He was also found to be good at
gymnastics but indifferent to anything else. He began truanting and
frequenting Angelo Baptiste's shop near Seven Steps, returning to
Zonnebloem only for English composition and physical education.

One day the police arrived at their flat to investigate cases of
50 continuous pilfering from the shop, reported by Mr Baptiste. Milton
escaped by climbing over the back wall and for the next three days he
lay low and slept in the storeroom of the very shopkeeper who had
reported him. Baptiste's losses increased drastically during this period,
until the police surprised Milton late one night while he was sleeping

---

8 **repairman-cum-bouncer**: Handwerker und Rausschmeißer in einem   17 **tight**:
strict   19 **rickety**: klapprig   21 **for old times' sake**: um der schönen Erinnerung
Willen   23–24 **gather around**: form a group   33 **penchant for**: fondness for,
liking for   34 **maiden aunt**: unmarried aunt   37 **scold sb.**: jdn. tadeln   **clout
sb.**: beat sb.   38 **officialdom**: bureaucracy   44 **avid**: very keen   **startling**:
surprising   46 **truant** (v): not go to school   50 **pilfer**: steal   52 **lay low**: hide

under some hessian sacks next to the macaroni. He got off lightly with a hiding which was approved by his mother, administered by a burly sergeant in the charge office.

His skill in physical education now came to the fore and he soon became the best tap-dancer in Sterling Street Flats. His ambition 5 stretched beyond such narrow horizons and he began performing to admiring spectators on the Grand Parade, with his cap strategically placed on the ground in front of him for donations. His dexterity helped when any policeman appeared on the scene. Milton, while tapping, could lean down and without losing his balance scoop up the cap and 10 coins with one deft movement of the arm and hand. He would then run like hell for Castle Bridge. He got away with this strategy countless times until two enterprising policemen put an end to it. While one approached him cautiously, the other waited at Castle Bridge. Late that night he was released into the custody of his long-suffering mother after he had 15 dazzled the officers on duty with a display of tap-dancing and had even sent his cap around for donations.

After he left school voluntarily, to the relief of his teacher aunt, he spent much of his time watching gangster movies in Star Bioscope. Late one afternoon he decided to put his new-found interest into practice. 20 He covered his mouth and nose with a scarf the way James Cagney did in films, borrowed Byron's raincoat and with a realistic toy gun he had pilfered from a stall on the Grand Parade, entered Angelo's shop when he calculated it would be empty of customers. Instead of taking fright and handing over all his takings as they did in the movies, Angelo 25 laughed fit to kill himself and then knocked Milton out cold with a huge bottle of olive oil. Milton was not seriously hurt but found himself behind bars and soaked in oil for the first time in his life. He was found guilty and sent to the local reformatory.

It was while there, since his movements were drastically restricted, 30 that he developed his literary ability. Having the name Milton he was assigned to work in the reform school library and began reading and writing during his spare time. He was on occasions a star turn at concerts and dazzled the spectators with his dextrous footwork, but his real reputation rested on the fact that he wrote highly original and innovative 35 as well as libellous verse. Boys paid him with cigarettes to write poems about warders they disliked and Milton was able to churn these out

almost at will. He seemed to know all the unsavoury gossip about
everyone. This peculiar upsurge in literary appreciation on the part of
40 his charges soon attracted the attention of the superintendent, and when
a few of these poems actually reached his desk he realised that he had a
serious problem on his hands. Seldom had he come across such smut,
such filth, such libel, rather jaggedly written but highly original. Milton,
although he vehemently denied authorship, was placed in the
45 punishment cell for two weeks, and spent his time composing scurrilous
poems about the superintendent. After his release from the cell a poem
was found pinned to the door of the administration office. It described
the superintendent's sexual life in the most embarrassing detail. The
superintendent laid down an ultimatum to his superiors: either Milton
50 went or he did. As Milton still had two more years to serve and the
authorities were reluctant to release him, the superintendent was granted
a transfer to Beaufort West.

Milton proved the power of the pen. No man harmed him with
impunity. Defamatory verses flowed from him and were always found
55 posted up in the most strategic places. There was a general sigh of relief
from the officials when his sentence was over. The new superintendent,
having been forewarned by his predecessor, refused Milton permission
to read his valedictory poem to the assembly.

His longing for certain forms of education but loathing for educational
60 institutions remained permanently with him. He got a job as caretaker
of his old school, where his maiden aunt was still teaching and the

1 **hessian**: Sackleinen   2 **hiding** (n): beating   **burly**: strongly built   4 **come to
the fore**: play a more important role   6 **stretch beyond**: go further than   10 **scoop
sth. up**: pick sth. up   11 **deft**: skilful   13 **enterprising**: unusually clever
15 **custody**: Obhut   21 **James Cagney**: US film star who often played gangsters
24 **take fright**: be frightened   29 **reformatory**: youth prison   32 **assign sb. to
sth.**: jdm. etwas zuweisen   33 **star turn**: high point   36 **libellous** ['laɪbələs]:
untrue and damaging   37 **churn sth. out**: produce sth. easily and in large numbers
38 **unsavoury gossip**: widerwärtiger Tratsch   39 **upsurge**: sudden increase
42 **smut**: 'dirty' writing   45 **scurrilous**: unflätig   50 **two more years to serve**: a
further two years in prison   53–54 **with impunity**: without being punished
54 **defamatory**: intended to harm the reputation of others   58 **valedictory**:
farewell   59 **loathing**: deep hate   60 **caretaker**: person who looks after a building

principal who had scolded him on his first day was still the head. During his spare time he read whatever English setwork books he found abandoned in classrooms and continued his poetry career. The principal was uneasy about the attraction he seemed to have for the Standard Six class, who spent their intervals clustered around the caretaker's room 5 listening to him reciting his latest works. It was very commendable to have so creative a caretaker but he was proving just a bit too popular.

Milton's job came to an abrupt end when the police raided a notorious shebeen in Ayre Street and picked up not only Milton but half a dozen chairs and tables missing from the school. Milton was allowed out on 10 bail, which his mother persuaded the reluctant maiden aunt to pay. The principal handed in a sworn affidavit implicating Milton. One morning a scurrilous poem describing details of the principal's private life was found pinned up on the pupils' noticeboard. By the time it was discovered, hastily handwritten copies were circulating among the 15 Standard Sixes. The author of the original work remained anonymous but the English teacher claimed to recognise the style as Miltonic.

This time Milton was sentenced to three years in Roeland Street jail for theft of state property. The principal went on early retirement. Milton's reputation preceded him in prison so that while serving his 20 sentence he was allowed no writing material whatsoever. His mother died during this period and his brothers dispersed in different directions. When Milton came out he was alone in the world, so accepted a job at Mary's and moved into her spare backroom. During the day he was general handyman and during the evenings acted as bouncer. 25

He still practised his dancing on occasions, entertaining The Girls with his fancy footwork. He entered for the annual talent contest at Star Bioscope and, dressed in the latest fashion, the Zoot suit, appeared on stage to do his number. He looked smart in a check suit with padded shoulder, narrow waist, knee-length coat and trousers tapering at the 30 ankles. He wore huge black-and-white Jarmans with dancing-studs knocked into the toes and heels. Mary and The Girls took the evening off to root for him as he jived his way to victory. The compère referred to him glowingly as Zoot, the Jive King of District Six, and the name stuck. The Miltonic era was over. 35

Number 203, the cottage next door to Mary's, was originally occupied by Mr and Mrs Punch Davids, an elderly, pale and fragile couple who spent their last days quietly drinking themselves to death. They were in a permanent state of intoxication and had no idea who their neighbours

40 were and anyway couldn't care less. They had one married daughter who lived in Walmer Estate and occasionally paid them worried visits. Mr Punch Davids followed the same ritual every day. Just before Bernstein's Bottle Store opened at 9 a.m. he opened his cottage door and unsteadily wheezed his way down the street, clutching two empty

45 bottles close to his thin chest. He was on his way to get his daily supplies. He always bought one bottle of whisky and another of Old Brown Sherry. Nobody ever determined which was for whom or whether the couple shared the bottles and mixed their drinks. Nor did anyone ever discover where they found the money, but it was rumoured that Mr

50 Davids had been a successful second-hand car salesman in his time and had retired on a reasonable pension. Having received his supplies he would amble back erratically, shut his door and draw the curtains. Mrs Punch Davids was seldom seen except when on rare occasions she was forced to shop for food. The following morning her husband repeated

55 his odyssey to Bernstein's. Neighbours referred to this as the Wine Route. On Saturdays he bought a double supply to last over the weekend.

In the early hours of one Saturday morning Zoot was locking up at Mary's when he saw smoke pouring out of the back window of 203. He alerted Mary, who sent The Butterfly to wake up Moodley in order to

60 phone for the Fire Brigade. The rest of The Girls filled buckets with water and tried to douse the fire. Zoot tied a wet handkerchief around his nose and mouth and smashed his way through the front door. He firstly dragged Mrs Davids through the billowing smoke. She was in her nightdress, badly asphyxiated and clutching an empty glass. Then he

65 returned and brought out Mr Davids, very drunk and somewhat

6 **commendable**: lobenswert   8 **notorious**: famous for being bad   9 **shebeen** [ʃɪ'biːn] (SAE): cheap bar   10-11 **on bail**: auf Kaution   12 **sworn affidavit** [ˌæfɪ'deɪvɪt]: eidesstattliche Erklärung   17 **miltonic**: in the style of the poet Milton 22 **disperse**: sich verstreuen   29 **padded**: gepolstert   30 **taper**: become narrower 33 **root for sb.**: cheer sb., support sb.   39 **intoxication**: drunkenness   44 **wheeze**: breathe heavily   52 **amble**: walk slowly   **erratic**: (here) not in a straight line 61 **douse sth.** [daʊz]: put sth. (esp. a fire) out with water   63 **billowing smoke**: clouds of smoke   64 **asphyxiate**: ersticken   **clutch sth.**: hold sth. tightly

scorched. When the couple were out of danger, with their few sticks of furniture standing undamaged on the pavement, the Fire Brigade roared down from Roeland Street with all bells ringing.

When Mr and Mrs Punch Davids were dismissed from hospital where they had been treated for minor burns and shock, their Walmer Estate daughter fetched them and placed them in an old-age home in Bokmakierie. The cottage now stood empty and abandoned. The back-room had partially collapsed but the front section was relatively intact except for some blackened walls and gaping holes where the windows and door had been.

One day Zoot decided to pay Katzen, who owned the cottage, a business call. He put on his fashionable check suit and his Jarmans with dancing-studs in the heels and toes and strolled down to the shop in Hanover Street.

'I am very glad to see that you are enjoying good health,' he said by way of introduction.

Katzen waited for the next move.

'I am very glad for you in spite of the fact that you could have suffered a great loss. It is sad when one of one's cottages almost burns down.'

Kathen's suspicions were growing.

'You know I felt I was obliged to rescue Mr and Mrs Davids because that is what one ought to do if it is necessary. One must always help others if one can.'

Katzen reluctantly agreed although he felt the barb was directed at him.

'Think of what could have happened to those good people if they had been burnt to death in your house.'

'It wasn't my fault that the house caught fire.'

'And if my guardian angel had not told me that your house was on fire, those good people would not be living now.'

Katzen drew a deep breath but remained silent.

'And what would everyone have said? Whom would everyone have blamed? I will tell you. I will suggest that they would have said "It is the fault of the owner of the cottages. He hired it to them but did not think to protect them from harm. He lives comfortably and all he thinks of is his rent." They could have said that.'

'But that would not be true!'

'And perhaps those same people who say those untrue things will go to the police and say the same to the police and ask them to investigate why those good people were allowed to drink all the time in the owner's house and he never paid them any attention.'

'What do you want?' Katzen abruptly changed the subject and resigned himself to the worst.

'I really want to be friends with you. I want us to reach a pleasant agreement. I will offer to move into the burnt-out shell of a house and fix it up and make it safe for people to live in, even old people who drink a lot without anyone caring. And in addition I will pay you rent every end of the month.'

'And where will you get money from to pay the rent?'

'Every end of the month I shall come to you at this shop and I shall say to you, "Friend Katzen," I will say, "here is your rent," and then you will give me a receipt and you will sign your name on it.'

Katzen knew that there was absolutely no chance of ever getting any rent and, once Zoot moved in, absolutely no chance of ever getting rid of him.

'I am not sure. I will need some time to think about it.'

'And then while you are thinking, perhaps I will write a poem about it. I have not written a poem for a long time. Perhaps my guardian angel will inspire me to write a poem about fires and people who are nearly burnt to death and landlords that don't really care and what other people say.'

Zoot moved in the following week and bought a bed, table and four chairs from Katzen on hire-purchase. He promised to pay the first instalment of the furniture on the same day he paid the first month's rent. Katzen sighed and had the furniture delivered. It was no real loss as the articles were second-hand and had been repossessed from a family in Kewtown who had already paid off three-quarters of the instalments.

---

1 **scorched**: burnt on the outside   9 **gaping**: wide open   24 **barb**: insulting remark   43 **resign yourself to the worst**: prepare for sth. very bad
64 **instalment**: monthly payment   66 **repossess sth.**: take sth. back because it was not fully paid for

The Jungle Boys

The Abrahams family lived at 205 Caledon Street, the third cottage in Buckingham Palace. Their house was somewhat cramped because it was occupied by Mr Suleiman Abrahams, his wife Sies Mariam, their three enormous and powerful grown-up sons, Amaai, Toyer and Braima, and their only daughter Moena. The family always sat in the small dining-room during the evenings, when the boys played their jazz records on the radiogram which dominated it. 5

Mr Suleiman Abrahams was a small ineffectual man who seldom spoke and whose wife never allowed him to take any decisions. He owned a tailor's shop next to Last-Knight's barber's shop and on any day of the week could be seen through the plateglass window, wearing an *onder kuffiyeh* and sitting sewing barefooted and crosslegged on a low table. His wooden *kaparrings* were always next to him on the floor. At home he spent the evenings in his dining-room, immersed in the *Cape Times* and *Argus*, reading right through the noise of his wife's chatter and the loud music from the radiogram. He seemed oblivious of any distraction. His wife had previously been Christian and baptised Miriam. But when she married Mr Abrahams she changed to the Muslim faith and was known from then onwards as Sies Mariam. She was as noisy as her husband was quiet and after years of reprimanding him because of his lack of ambition she finally gave up, ignored him completely, and focused her interests on her sons and daughter. Mr Abrahams did not seem to mind. 10 15 20

The family had originally lived in Rose Street in the Bo-Kaap. The three boys, then already huge while still teenagers, were notorious for their strength and taciturnity. Their method of deciding any dispute was to use hands, feet and teeth if necessary. This gained them the nickname of the Jungle Boys, which stuck with them even after they were grown-up and the family had lived in Caledon Street for many years. 25

Soon after moving into Buckingham Palace Mr Abrahams, to drown the incessant noise of his wife's speaking, bought the largest and loudest radiogram he could find, on hire-purchase from his new landlord, Katzen. He also bought the boys the noisiest jazz records on the market. The neighbours all turned out in force to watch it being manoeuvred 30

35 into place in the dining-room. When it was finally installed with everyone standing around admiringly, Sies Mariam, in a flowing red-satin gown she had persuaded her husband to make for the occasion, stood poised to initiate the radiogram by playing the first record. This was when Braima, the youngest Jungle, a dirty, tousle-headed fourteen-
40 year-old at the time, for some inexplicable reason proceeded to bite a large piece out of its leg with his teeth. His brothers silently admired. The Jungle Boys were like that.

They had one sister, Moena, who was small, timid and extremely plain. She helped her mother at home and seldom went out other than
45 to Star Bioscope on rare occasions with her mother or to Green Point common with her father when her brothers were playing rugby for the Young Anemones.

The boys experienced a pugnacious and silent childhood. They hunted and attacked in a pack and already at an early age showed both
50 mean and generous streaks. They left school in Bo-Kaap at the primary level, or rather they were forced to leave when they marched into Moena's class and beat up her teacher in front of the pupils because he had dared to make nasty references to her looks. They were like that.

The spokesman for the three, when it became absolutely necessary,
55 was the eldest, Amaai. The remaining two never disagreed with him but followed almost intuitively in taking any collective action there was to take.

Amaai was a driver for Globe Furnishers; Toyer was already a *sarang*, or foreman, at the Docks; and Braima was a fruit hawker. They seldom
60 mixed with anyone in the street other than with Zoot and The Boys. Mrs Abrahams on the contrary spoke to anyone who would listen to her.

---

2 **cramped**: too small, narrow   7 **radiogram**: (formerly) cabinet with a radio and a record player   8 **ineffectual**: zaghaft   12 **onder kuffiyeh**: headscarf
13 **kaparrings** (SAE): type of wooden sandals   16 **oblivious**: unaware
20 **reprimand sb.**: tell sb. off   26 **taciturnity** [ˌtæsɪ'tɜːnəti]: quality of hardly ever speaking   31 **incessant**: that never stops   37 **gown**: expensive dress
39 **tousle-headed**: with uncombed/unruly hair   40 **inexplicable**: that cannot be explained   43 **timid**: shy   46 **common** (n): land open to the public
48 **pugnacious**: wanting to fight   50 **mean and generous streaks**: good and bad sides

The Jungle Boys spent most evenings either playing jazz records on the gram or at Winsor Park playing dominoes or cards with Zoot and his boarders. Sometimes they would sit smoking quietly while Zoot and Pretty-Boy discussed and argued about politics, philosophy and how whites treated the coloured people. If there was any trouble, Zoot could 5 rely on the Jungles and, if the latter needed any assistance, which was highly unlikely, they were sure they could rely on Zoot and The Boys.

The Jungle Boys' only physical recreation other than fighting was rugby. The three formed the formidable font-rank of the Young Anemones Rugby Football Club's first-team scrum. They practised in 10 Trafalgar Park and played hard and dirty. They turned up regularly with their team to fulfil fixtures but these seldom materialised because most of the teams they were scheduled to play would rather forfeit the match than meet the Jungle Boys head-on. They had that sort of reputation. It was only at the semi-final stages that they found themselves challenged 15 by other forwards as huge and as dirty-playing as they were.

The last final was against Summer Roses, a team which also enjoyed a formidable reputation. Amaai had spotted the referee the evening before, slipping into Mary's for some pre-match recreation. When he came out much later that night, Amaai was there waiting for him and 20 suggested laconically that he was not very happy about a match being refereed by a person who had such questionable morals. He could be happier if such a referee were to turn his obvious bias in the direction of the Young Anemones on the following day. He also suggested that he could get his learned friend Mr Zoot September to compose a poem on 25 the theme of free sex and sport not mixing particularly well. Just before the match was about to start, the referee reported to the President of the Rugby Union that he had been threatened but refused to give names or details. The President had both teams lined up in front of him on the field and in front of all the spectators gave them a tongue-lashing over 30 the microphone.

If anything this aggravated an already tense situation. One thing both teams now had in common was an intense dislike for the referee from whom they had been told by the President the complaint had come. The match was played at a furious pace. Before the end two Young Anemones 35 and one Summer Rose as well as a drunk spectator had been sent to out-patients for treatment. Fortunately Somerset Hospital was on the

other side of a fence so the stretchers could be passed through a hole in the palings. There was no final result because there was no final whistle
40 because the referee was also transported through the opening in the fence on a stretcher. The scrum wheeled suddenly and collapsed on him when he least expected it. And when the players rose the referee did not rise with them. Although the result was undecided, all declared that for the Jungle Boys it was a great and famous victory. They played like
45 that.

---

2 **gram**: radiogram   3 **boarder**: Untermieter   10 **scrum**: Gedränge   13 **schedule** (v): plan   **forfeit sth.** ['fɔːfɪt]: etwas kampflos verlieren   23 **bias** ['baɪes]: prejudice, support for one side   30 **tongue-lashing**: Rüffel   37 **out-patients**: Ambulanz
38 **stretcher**: Trage   39 **palings** (pl): Bretterzaun   41 **wheel** (v): turn around

Pretty-Boy

When Zoot moved into 203 he was uncomfortable but happy. Most of the rooms in the cottage still remained intact except for smoke marks on the walls. There was a front stoep that led into the dining-room. From this ran two bedrooms, off one of which was the toilet and bathroom which had no bath. Off the other ran a small kitchen and finally a back-room which led onto the porch. It was this back-room that had been most damaged in the fire. It was used to store empties and Mr Punch Davids used to fall asleep there on his way to fetch replacements. A yard fenced in with rusty corrugation determined the boundaries of the property.

Zoot scrubbed and scraped as much of the smoke marks off the walls and ceilings as he could, and neatly stacked the empty whisky and Old Brown Sherry bottles in the broken-down back-room. He shored up all openings such as doors and windows with wood he found at the early-morning market. He then placed the table and chairs in the dining-room, and the bed in the first bedroom, which would be his. Mary presented him with a set of linen for the bed and The Girls brought doilies they had crocheted for the table. Zoot was now proudly settled in his own home.

One night late, when he had just come home from Mary's, he was surprised to find that the planks shutting the back door had been removed. He entered cautiously and heard the unmistakable sound of snoring coming from his bedroom. In the dark he could make out someone sleeping on his bed. He hit out viciously and had to do so several more times before a body stirred and rolled down onto the floor. Then it sat up and rubbed its eyes. Zoot lit the lamp. He was amazed to see Pretty-Boy Vermeulen.

'What the hell are you doing in my bed? And how the hell did you get into my house?'

'I removed the planks from your back door, my friend Zoot. I am very sleepy now so I wish you will leave me alone.'

'Weren't you supposed to be living somewhere in Jo'burg?'

'Allow me to rise from the floor and I will explain. I will tell you all.'

Zoot took the lamp and led Pretty-Boy into the dining-room.

35 'My friend Zoot is a wealthy man, I can see. He has a mansion of a house.'

'Cut out the nonsense. What do you want here?'

'I have been living in Johannesburg for many years, as you know –
for almost all the years since I last saw you in the reformatory. Now and
40 then I also lived at Pretoria Central but most times I was in Fordsburg.
This is really a very beautiful house. My friend must be very rich. He
must have come into much money.'

'Why the hell did you come to Cape Town? You are on holiday, I
suppose.'

45 'No, I am not on holiday, my friend. Things were beginning to get
very uncomfortable and I did not like the boarding facilities at Pretoria
jail. The food there was not very good. I have come all this way specially
to visit the friend of my youth. I heard from many that he was wealthy, a
famous writer and owned a beautiful house.'

50 'I am not wealthy or famous, and do not own this house. I pay rent
for it to a miser of a landlord.'

Zoot omitted to mention that he had not paid Katzen anything since
he had moved in months before.

'Then, if you will allow me,' Pretty-Boy continued, 'I will move in
55 with you and help you to pay the rent to that miser of a landlord.'

Pretty-Boy had received his nickname at the reformatory where he had
first met Zoot. He was bronze with black curly hair, well-cut features
and striking blue, innocent eyes. He was born in Johannesburg of an
Afrikaner father and his brown servant. He looked younger than he
60 really was and his eyes always made women feel strong urges to believe
in him. He never raised any objections to that.

---

9 **corrugation**: Wellblech   11 **scrub and scrape sth.**: etwas abschrubben und
abkratzen   12 **stack sth.**: etwas stapeln   13 **shore sth. up**: support sth.
17 **linen**: bed sheets   18 **doily**: Spitzendeckchen   **crochet sth.** [ˈkreʊʃeɪ]: etwas
häkeln   24 **vicious** [ˈvɪʃəs]: brutal   25 **stir**: move   32 **Jo'burg**: Johannesburg
40 **Pretoria Central, Fordsburg**: prisons   42 **come into sth.**: inherit sth.
51 **miser** [ˈmaɪzə]: Geizhals   57 **curly**: lockig   60 **urge** (n): desire

What Zoot could do with his feet, Pretty-Boy could do with his hands. His fingers were long and flexible. This was one part of his body he cared for. He could repair any broken gadget, open any locked door and pickpocket any unsuspecting victim. He always, however, maintained a rigid code of personal honour. He stole only from those he   5
disliked or he reckoned could afford it, and gave generously to anyone he felt needed it. His recklessness and bravado reached such a stage that the first time he was caught was in a shop in Doornfontein when he was counting the notes in a victim's pocket before extracting them. He was sent to reformatory in the Cape, where he soon teamed up with Zoot,   10
whom he then worshipped. When his term was over he left with an extra set of clothes he had appropriated and the chief warder's wrist-watch in case he found it necessary to tell the time.

For the next few years he lived either in Fordsburg or in Pretoria Central Prison until his unexpected appearance at Zoot's cottage.   15
Although dirty and unkempt from his journey, he was still as handsome and innocent-looking as ever.

'Yes, I will help you, friend Zoot, to pay the rent. Look, I did not come empty-handed. I have brought you these pictures as a present for your cottage all the way from Jo'burg and this bottle of the finest whisky   20
on the market.'

He produced four framed and mounted reproductions of King George VI and his queen, which seemed to indicate that he had not just arrived in Cape Town. He also held up a dusty bottle of White Horse whisky.   25

'I think we should drink to our reunion, my friend Zoot. You must first drink this fine whisky and then you must write a poem about our meeting. I am sure you are a famous writer already.'

Zoot left without saying a word to borrow two glasses from Mary.

After much argument and calculation, they reached an agreement.   30
Pretty-Boy would occupy the second bedroom and pay the rent to Zoot at the end of every month. No-one bothered to discuss how much the rent was. Pretty-Boy also promised to fit in a proper door and windows to the cottage.

Food was now no longer a problem. When necessary he would go   35
downtown and return with pizzas in large, flat cardboard containers, or cartons of curry and rice. Once he brought home the curry still hot in its

pot. Zoot began to look forward to a second dinner late every evening when he returned from Mary's. Every meal procured by Pretty-Boy was an epicurean surprise.

One evening Pretty-Boy was waiting for him at the door.

'I have a surprise for you, friend Zoot. You must close your eyes and allow me to lead you into our house.'

He led a reluctant Zoot into the kitchen.

'Now you may open your eyes.'

There stood a fridge, brand new though dented on one side.

'I got it from a friend at a bargain price.'

'And where did you get the money from to pay this friend a bargain price?'

'Let me put it to you this way. Had I found the need to pay my friend it would have been a bargain price.'

'And what do we do with this fridge when we have no electricity?'

'I have thought about that also, my friend Zoot. When the time is right and they have switched off all the outside lights, I will lead the electricity into our cottage.'

'From the City Council?'

'From the City Council.'

'Are you serious?'

'And we will use it for our stove also.'

'What stove?'

'Tomorrow, or maybe the day after, I shall also get a stove from my friend at a bargain price.'

The inside of the house began to take on a distinctly domestic shape. In the kitchen the fridge and stove were now connected. There was a new radiogram playing in the dining-room and Pretty-Boy had fixed lights in every room.

---

3 **gadget**: small piece of household equipment   7 **recklessness**: without thinking of any danger   **bravado** [brə'vɑːdəʊ]: Prahlerei   11 **worship sb.**: treat sb. like a god   12 **appropriate sth.**: take sth. without permission   16 **unkempt**: with uncombed hair   39 **procure sth.**: get sth.   40 **epicurean** [ˌepɪkjuˈrɪən]: gourmet   47 **at a bargain price**: very cheap

'The meter-reader from the Council will not check our house since we have no meter. We have established an understanding.'

The outside also improved and Pretty-Boy fitted in doors and windows, all received from the friend at a bargain price.

The meals Zoot received at night were now not only choice but also hot. Sometimes it would be a piece of boiled haddock, at other times a warm salome or a fried chop. They always ate in absolute silence until Pretty-Boy made the coffee. They would then retire to the dining-room and between sips discuss whatever problems there were, or just talk about anything.

'I have been thinking, my friend Zoot, we must now paint this cottage on the inside as well as on the outside. We must also give this house a name. It is not enough that it is known as 203. It is a special house. And the name must be printed right next to the new front door. It is not fitting that a man like my friend, Zoot September, should live in such a house which also has no name.'

Zoot sipped at his coffee and then asked slowly, 'And where will we find the paint to paint the house? Do you expect me to go to that miser of a landlord and say, "Mr Katzen, I would like some paint to paint my house"? Do you not think he will then remind me of the rent I owe him? My guardian angel only knows that I cannot pay the rent to him unless those who owe me rent first pay me.'

Pretty-Boy ignored the obvious reference.

'And also, if we do get the paint, then who will do the painting? Those of us who work hard during the day will be far too tired at night. Maybe those who do not work so hard during the day and only walk around the Grand Parade can do the painting.'

Pretty-Boy wanted to remind him of the doors and windows but decided not to do so. Zoot was in a mean mood.

'That also is no problem. I have yet another friend who can do it. He is a master painter.'

'And I suppose you also have a master name-giver who will give us a name for this house?'

'No, that I have already thought about. I hear that these cottages are called Buckingham Palace. That is a fit place for royal families. But this house must be called Windsor Park for that is where a king like my friend Zoot September lives.'

Although Zoot felt flattered he was a bit uneasy.

'And when will the paint and the painter come?' he asked hesitantly.

40 'As soon as I can make the arrangements. You must leave all this to me and my friend. I have a reliable friend as you must have noticed.'

The following evening when Zoot came home there was a warm gammon steak waiting for him. In the kitchen stood a ten-gallon drum of bright pink paint.

45 'It is the only colour my friend could find. There is nothing wrong with the house of a king being painted pink. My friend told me there is more where this came from but unfortunately all the same colour.'

'And what about the painter?'

'He is sleeping on the back porch.'

50 The following morning Zoot was introduced to Oubaas. He was grizzled and bent and said nothing but grinned toothlessly at everything. Pretty-Boy explained that Oubaas was a qualified master painter but did not elaborate on his qualifications. He also mentioned something about his losing his last job, decades ago, because of some misunderstanding.

55 He had since been living on the Grand Parade until Pretty-Boy had met him and commissioned him to do the work.

Oubaas was prepared to paint the house in return for temporary board and lodging. He was half-deaf and at times Pretty-Boy had to shout instructions to him.

60 'Oubaas, you must paint all the outside and the inside. Do you understand? You must start as soon as I come back from town. I am going to get you brushes and a ladder. I have a friend who can get me these things.'

Oubaas grinned toothlessly. Pretty-Boy left for the Grand Parade and

65 Zoot went to work at Mary's. After Pretty-Boy had returned with the implements Oubaas worked happily singing and humming to himself. When Zoot came home that evening the outside walls glowed a warm

---

5 **choice**: very good quality   6 **haddock**: Schellfisch   7 **salome**: salami   29 **mean**: bad   43 **gammon**: type of pork meat   51 **grizzled**: grey-haired   56 **commission sb.**: give sb. a particular task (for payment)   58 **board and lodging**: somewhere to eat and sleep   66 **hum**: summen

pink. He was a bit perturbed to find that Oubaas had painted the doors and window frames also pink.

The following day Oubaas worked on the inside. Zoot was now confident about his ability and came back that night in a happy mood. Pretty-Boy was waiting for him outside, a sure sign of trouble or a surprise waiting for him. 5

When they entered Zoot was horrified as he surveyed the lounge. The walls and ceiling were bright pink. So were the table, chairs and radiogram. Zoot walked through to the pink kitchen. The fridge and stove shone pink. 10

'Oh my God,' moaned Zoot.

'Wait till you see your bed.'

'Where is that moron now?'

'Sleeping on the back porch.'

'Is that pink also?' 15

'Yes.'

'I think he must be taught a lesson.'

Zoot kicked Oubaas awake but he was such a pathetic figure grinning foolishly that all Zoot could say to Pretty-Boy was, 'Tomorrow you and this idiot get some rags and turps from your friend in Cape Town and 20 get the bloody paint off the kitchen stuff.'

'And your bed?'

'And my bed.'

'And the table, chairs and gram?'

'And the table, chairs and gram.' 25

Pretty-Boy and Oubaas spent the next few days rubbing, scraping and washing and managed to restore most of the furniture to their former state. The fridge and stove still retained a pink glow and Zoot resigned himself to sleeping on a pink bed.

Pretty-Boy's education had been very limited and he was not good at 30 spelling. Zoot returned one evening to find WINSOR PARK printed boldly in blue next to the pink door. And so it remained ever afterwards.

Oubaas took up permanent residence in the tumble-down back-room after Pretty-Boy had negotiated on his behalf. 35

'I have told him that every end of the month he must pay the rent to me which I will in turn add to mine and give to you so that you can pay that miser of a landlord.'

It was The Butterlfy who suggested that Winsor Park have a house-
40 warming party. The idea was taken up by everyone except Zoot.
'That miser of a Katzen will say that if we can afford a party then we can afford to pay his rent. Perhaps he will even tell the Council about the lights. He is that sort of man.'
'We shall invite him also,' Pretty-Boy replied. 'We shall send him an invitation in an envelope. You must write a poem to invite him. Maybe
45 his hard heart will melt when he sees how pretty we have made his house.'
Mary donated most of the booze. Zoot managed to find the rest. Pretty-Boy began piling up refreshments in the fridge and stove. The Girls baked koeksisters and fried samoosas. Oubaas helped to put up
50 streamers and balloons. Everyone in the street was invited. Many more came. At 6 a.m. the police declared the party closed.
It had been a tremendous success and everyone drifted home bleary-eyed and happy. Zoot was snoring loudly in his bed. Pretty-Boy was sleeping under the dining-room table. Oubaas was curled up on the
55 back porch clutching an empty gin bottle to his chest. Early in the party a powerful man with a thick, red beard had drifted in from outside. No-one knew who he was or who had invited him. Even better, no-one cared. He was now sitting fast asleep on the toilet seat. Boere stayed on for the next few years.

13 **moron**: idiot; stupid person   18 **pathetic**: armselig   20 **rags**: Lumpen   **turps**: turpentine   34 **tumble-down**: heruntergekommen   35 **negotiate**: come to an agreement   **on his behalf**: for him   50 **streamers**: Luftschlangen   52–53 **bleary-eyed**: with tired eyes   54 **curl up**: roll up

Mr Wilkens

Although they never openly showed it, the Jungle Boys doted on their sister Moena and jealously protected her. Nobody knew from what. Their concern was totally unnecessary since no man in the District had ever thought even remotely of making a pass at her. She was not ugly but inordinately plain and was never noticed. She in her turn doted on 5 her brothers and, when she found the opportunity, was understanding and solicitous towards anyone who needed help. This seldom happened. Besides being homely she was also very shy.

Life changed suddenly for almost all at 205 when a cousin from Kimberley moved in to stay. Only Mr Abrahams seemed unaffected. The 10 newcomer was a very fair, pretty and vivacious girl, the same age as Moena. She also, confusingly, had the same name. She was fully aware of her good looks and soon proved to be an outrageous coquette. Her father had sent her to his brother in Cape Town so that she could find work but more so in order to get her away from the boys in her home- 15 town. It was arranged that while looking for a suitable job she would board with Boeta Suleiman Abrahams and his family, who had been entreated to keep a watchful eye over her sometimes dubious behaviour.

It was confusing having two girls of the same name and almost the 20 same age in one house. The family simply referred to them as 'Onse Moena' and 'Moena van Kimberley' but the neighbours called the cousin Moena Mooies and the Abrahams girl Moena Lelik. They would never dare call 'Onse Moena' this in front of her family as they knew the Jungle Boys' reputation for suddenly turning nasty. The Kimberley Moena was 25 flattered and tried everything in her power to live up to her nickname, usually at the expense of her plain cousin. Onse Moena could not see through her cousin's wiles and loved and supported her vanities.

Moena Mooies did absolutely nothing about procuring a job and spent much of her time lolling about the house, trying on her cousin's 30 make-up and playing the Jungle Boys' records when they were at work. She soon became friendly with Mary and The Girls and visited the Casbah regularly, especially when she was bored. Her aunt was worried about this new development and scolded and threatened but it only

35 served to make her more resolute and determined. Amaai was all for giving her a good hiding but Moena Lelik gently dissuaded him. She was the only person capable of reasoning with her brothers when they were determined on something. They decided to ignore Moena Mooies. Now only Moena Lelik and her mother spoke to her, an arrangement
40 she found quite satisfactory.

A flashy Dodge, all shiny cream with black trimmings, was sometimes seen parked late at night outside Mary's house. One Saturday afternoon, however, it came cruising slowly down Caledon Street, passed the Casbah, and stopped outside 205. Mr Anthony Wilkens stepped out
45 gingerly onto the pavement. White people seldom came into the District on Saturday afternoons. Those who did were usually policemen, government or City Council officials, and door-to-door salesmen and collectors. White people also seldom paid social calls. Thus quite a few neighbours came out onto their stoeps at the unusual sight of Mr
50 Wilkens visiting the Abrahams family. The children playing in the street crowded and jostled around the car. Mr Wilkens shooed them away haughtily.

He was a rather pale man with mousy hair thick with brilliantine. He had a pencil-thin moustache. He was stylishly dressed in black blazer
55 and white flannels and wore shiny black-and-white shoes. He knocked ostentatiously at the door, which was opened just a little too soon by Sies Mariam, who had been peeping from behind the dining-room curtain. He asked in English whether Miss 'Mona' was in. He had come to call. He had met her at Miss Mary's and she had invited him.

---

1 **dote on sb.**: love sb. intensely   4 **make a pass at sb.**: flirt with sb.   7 **solicitous** [sə'lɪsɪtəs]: willing to help   8 **homely**: not attractive   11 **vivacious** [vɪ'veɪʃəs]: lebhaft   13 **outrageous** [aʊt'reɪdʒəs]: schamlos   18 **entreat sb.**: ask sb. intently
21 **onse** (Afrikaans): our   23 **mooies** (Afrikaans): pretty   **lelik** (Afrikaans): ugly
26 **live up to sth.**: etwas gerecht werden   28 **wile**: trick   **vanity**: Eitelkeit
30 **loll**: lie/hang around   36 **give sb. a good hiding**: beat sb.   **dissuade sb.**: convince sb. not to do sth.   37 **reason with sb.**: make sb. see sense
41 **trimmings**: Verzierungen   45 **gingerly**: behutsam   51 **jostle**: push one another   **shoo sb. away**: jdn. wegscheuchen   52 **haughty** ['hɔːti]: arrogant
53 **brilliantine**: pomade   56 **ostentatious**: demonstrativ   57 **peep**: look secretly

Moena had been waiting but nevertheless expressed surprise when the message was conveyed to her. She had spent the morning washing and curling her hair with the help of her cousin and had painted her face with Moena Lelik's best make-up. She had even prevailed on her cousin to lend her a new dress her father had just made for her. 5

Mr Wilkens was shown into the dining-room, where the Jungle Boys were listening to records on the gram, which still bore the scars of Braima's teeth. Mr Abrahams was sitting in a corner happily ignored, and immersed in his newspaper. Moena Mooies was called and came in all bashful and coy and very surprised although she had been watching 10 his arrival from the kitchen window. After she had ostensibly recovered she introduced her guest to the family. Mrs Abrahams was excited and said over and over again how honoured she was that a white man with a cream car was actually visiting her home. Moena Lelik was introduced and curtly ordered by her mother to go to the kitchen to prepare tea 15 ('Tea or coffee, Mr Wilkens? We're just a simple family') and koeksisters. She was admonished in Afrikaans to use the best tea service. The Jungle Boys nodded when introduced and returned to listening to records. Mr Abrahams mumbled some incoherent recognition and crept even deeper into his corner. 20

Mr Wilkens found himself talking only to a proud Moena and her admiring aunt. Although they seemed immersed in the jazz music, the boys were half-listening.

'Actually, like Miss Mona, I also originally came from Kimberley although from the other side of the tracks, so to speak. You know what 25 I mean, the white part. I find it so embarrassing when I'm with my Coloured friends to speak of the white section, because, unlike most of my Afrikaner friends, I really have no prejudices. I don't believe in all this apartheid nonsense. There are Coloureds and Malays like you who are working right under me in my shop. I especially like Malays. You 30 people are so law-abiding as I say all the time to my friends. And I simply love Malay music.' He addressed the boys. 'Do you have any of those Hollandse teams singing? They are so talented.'

Amaai gave him a long, hostile stare, then switched off the gram. He signalled to his brothers and they rose together and left the room without 35 a word to anyone.

'Oh dear, I hope that I have not annoyed them. Is it anything I said?'

Mrs Abrahams told him not to worry. The boys were like that.

'I love you people and your hospitable ways. You always make white
40 people like me so welcome. My people again are so stiff and reserved,
always thinking they are superior because of their colour. Give me
Coloureds and Malays any time, I always say to my friends. They never
fail to make one feel at home.'

Moena Lelik came in with a tray of tea and koeksisters.

45 'Ah, my favourite. I just love koeksisters. There's an Indian café near
my shop in Bree Street where I always buy mine.'

He informed them that he had worked as a salesman in Kimberley
before coming to Cape Town. He preferred the friendlier people in the
Mother City, the climate and the wonderful beaches. He was now
50 manager of a firm of outfitters in Long Street and would simply love to
employ Miss Mona as his personal secretary if only she could type and
do shorthand.

The following Saturday afternoon he picked her up by arrangement
and they drove off in the direction of Sea Point. He brought her home
55 early on Sunday morning, Moena Lelik having remained awake all night
to open the door for her cousin. After that Moena Mooies would be
picked up regularly every Saturday afternoon and sometimes stay away
until Sunday evening. She regaled Mrs Abrahams and her daughter with
accounts of expensive dinners in posh, whites-only restaurants, watching
60 movies in whites-only cinemas, and swimming off whites-only Clifton
Beach. Whenever he appeared at their home to pick her up, the Jungle
Boys left the room.

---

2 **convey sth. to sb.**: give sth. to sb.   4 **prevail on sb.**: persuade sb. to do sth.
7 **scar**: Narbe   9 **immersed in sth.**: completely involved in sth.   10 **bashful**: shy
coy: pretending to be shy   11 **ostensible**: apparent   15 **curtly**: in very few words
17 **admonish sb.**: advise sb. strongly   19 **incoherent** [ˌɪnkəʊˈhɪərənt]: barely under-
standable   19 **creep** (**crept – crept**): kriechen   25 **from the other side of the
tracks**: from a different (usu. richer or poorer) part of the city   31 **law-abiding**:
obeying the law   39 **hospitable** [hɒˈspɪtəbl]: welcoming to guests   52 **shorthand**:
Steno   58 **regale sb. with sth.**: entertain sb. with sth. (glamorous or exciting)
59 **posh** (infml): exclusive and expensive

One Saturday afternoon Amaai decided to wait for Mr Wilkens outside their home. As he was opening his car door Amaai slammed it shut and spoke to him through the open window.

'We don't want your type to come here in future.'

'May I ask why?' Mr Wilkens was surprised at the hostility in Amaai's voice. 5

'We don't like your kind.'

'Is it because I'm white?'

'No, it's because you're *you*.'

Mr Wilkens tried to force open the door but Amaai held it tight. 10

'Listen my man, take your hands away. This is my car. I have not come to see you. I have come to fetch Miss Mona.' He was very annoyed.

'Your seeing Miss Moena is not our business.'

'Well, in case you don't know it, we are now going steady.' 15

'That is also not our concern. But this house is. If you wish to see her in future you fetch her somewhere else. But you don't come here again, understand?'

'If you don't take your hands off my car I'll report you to the police. I'm not just one of your skollies you can treat anyhow.' 20

'We know you're a white man. You have told us so often enough. So, Mr White Man, if you ever come to this house again you're not going to be a Mr White Man for long afterwards.'

Mr Wilkens pressed the hooter until Moena Mooies appeared. Only then did Amaai let go his hold on the door and go back into the house, 25 ignoring her. The couple drove off at high speed.

When Moena returned late that night she found everyone still up and sitting in the dining-room except Mr Abrahams. Mr Wilkens had told her about Amaai's rude behaviour and she was now furious. They listened in silence as she swore, cursed and screamed in turn. Her cousin 30 tried her best to calm her. Mrs Abrahams was amazed at this tirade. The Jungle Boys seemed to ignore it and had their ears fixed on the music they were playing. When Moena could say no more she burst into tears. Amaai rose and switched off the gram.

'Before we go to sleep, we must have this thing out. This house is far 35 too small for all of us. What I told that white trash this afternoon was that he must never come here again for whatever reason. Now I'm telling

his girl-friend that there is no place for her in this house. Either she goes
or I go.'

40   The remaining brothers stood up.

'If Amaai goes then the two of us also go. And none of us are going.'

Toyer walked to the girls' room and returned with the suitcase Moena
Mooies had originally brought with her from Kimberley.

'Pack,' he said curtly, 'and go and live with that white rubbish of a
45   boy-friend in Sea Point or wherever he lives.'

Mrs Abrahams remained silent. She knew it would be unwise for her
to intervene when the boys were in such an ugly mood. Moena Lelik
tried to remonstrate but the boys ignored her.

'Go to your room,' Braima ordered Moena Mooies, and turning to his
50   sister, who was now also weeping, 'and you help her to pack.'

Moena Mooies decided that she would go to Mary's. Maybe later
during the week she would contact Mr Wilkens and they would then
decide on her future. She had partially recovered her composure and
was now surly and cocky. Without greeting anyone she left with her
55   cousin helping with her luggage. She slammed the door behind her.

The Dodge now fetched Moena Mooies at the Casbah. The Jungle Boys
behaved as if she did not exist although they saw her sometimes on the
stoep of 201. Mrs Abrahams was still curious about her niece and felt
guilty about the incident. She encouraged her daughter to visit Moena
60   Mooies and then report back to her.

The family were together in the dining-room one evening when
Moena Lelik returned from a secret visit to her cousin at Mary's. Her
mother noticed that she was upset and had been crying.

'What's the matter with the child?' she asked.

65   'It's about cousin Moena.'

'What about her? Is she sick or something?'

'Mr Wilkens has left her.'

---

15 **go steady**: fest zusammen sein   31 **tirade**: long angry speech   36 **white
trash**: poor white person/people   47 **ugly**: (here) dangerous   48 **remonstrate**:
protestieren   53 **recover your composure**: calm down   54 **surly**: unfriendly
cocky: a little arrogant

'And a good thing too. What a rubbish he has turned out to be.'

'He left her just like that. And she's going to have his baby.'

'How do you know all this?' Amaai asked without looking up.

'She told me so tonight.'

'So you've been seeing her?' There was a threat in his voice.

'Leave the child alone,' his mother said. 'So Moena's in trouble?'

'We must help her if we can. She needs money to get back to Kimberley. She only has us to turn to.'

Amaai spoke again. 'She does not deserve any help from us. She now has what she deserves. But God help that white trash whenever and wherever we lay our hands on him.'

The Jungle Boys raised no objection to Moena visiting her cousin and she now did so openly. Mrs Abrahams sent along little delicacies and comforts and started knitting for the baby to come. Two months later, Moena Lelik reported at dinner that there was not going to be a baby. Mary had made the arrangements. Moena Mooies had been very ill but was now almost fully recovered. The Jungle Boys appeared to show no interest and concentrated on listening to their music.

One evening Zoot was strolling back from Star Bioscope to Winsor Park. He decided to cross the dark field next to the church instead of walking up Clifton Hill and down Caledon Street. He spotted a cream Dodge discreetly parked in the shadow of the vestry wall where it could not easily be seen in the dark. He continued his leisurely stroll thinking deeply. Instead of going home he turned in at 205 and sat down in the dining-room where the Jungle Boys were as usual listening to records. Moena Lelik and her mother were busy in the kitchen and Mr Abrahams was already in bed.

'Good evening, my Jungle friends,' he began. 'I have not come to hear your beautiful music so late at night, but to bring you great tidings of joy.'

'What is it?' Amaai asked abruptly. He was always uncomfortable about Zoot's circumlocution.

'You know how I have often told you about my guardian angel. Perhaps you do not believe in my guardian angel because you do not understand my religion. But then again perhaps I am wrong and you also have a guardian angel. Perhaps there is such a thing as a Muslim guardian angel.'

'What are you trying to say?'

'I am trying to say, my Jungle friends, that as I was strolling over the
40 field next to our church, while I was strolling in deep thought, my Christian guardian angel pointed out something to me next to the vestry wall. You know how attached guardian angels are to churches. Perhaps Muslim guardian angels are just as attached to mosques.'

'Get on with it and cut the nonsense.'

45 'There, in the shadow of the vestry wall, I saw a certain car, a cream Dodge with black trimmings. My angel suggested to me that the owner might be in the near vicinity, maybe even at the Casbah, maybe even having tea with a certain lady whose name must not be mentioned in this house.'

50 Ammai rose with a determined look in his eyes. He switched off the music, took off the record, wiped it carefully and slipped it into its sleeve. Then he went into the yard and returned with a pickaxe handle and two crowbars. Zoot was still speaking.

'So I thought that such news should be conveyed immediately to my
55 dear Jungle friends. You see my guardian angel had told me that …'

'Come,' Amaai said cutting him short and handing a weapon to each of his brothers.

They crossed the field in silence and found the Dodge where Zoot had indicated it would be. Then they methodically started to smash the
60 windows and the bodywork. A crowd gathered and cheered on the destruction. The boys paid no attention to them. Someone must have reported what was happening at the Casbah because Mr Wilkens came rushing up waving a pistol, closely followed by Moena, Mary and The Girls. Zoot and The Boys also strolled over to watch. Mrs Abrahams and
65 her daughter stood on their stoep not daring to go nearer.

---

12 **raise no objection to sth.**: say nothing against sth.   21 **spot sth.**: notice sth.
22 **vestry**: Sakristei   29-30 **great tidings of joy** (biblical): wonderful news
32 **circumlocution**: Weitschweifigkeit   42 **attached to**: fond of   47 **vicinity**:
neighbourhood   52 **pickaxe handle**: Stiel einer Spitzhacke   53 **crowbar**:
Brechstange

Mr Wilkens looked at his wrecked car.

'My God, I'll make you pay for this, you bloody black bastards. This is what happens when one becomes too familiar with types like you.'

There were angry replies from the crowd to his outburst. Then Mr Wilkens geared into action and pointed his gun at the boys. Toyer 5 kicked hard and the gun sailed into the crowd and was never recovered again. Mr Wilkens now realised that it was best to make a run for it. Braima brought him down with a crash tackle. Then the boys went to work on him as they would the opposing front-rank in a rugby match. They tossed him from one brother to the other; they collapsed on him as 10 in a scrum; he was picked up and kicked from Braima to Amaai to Toyer. Although the crowd cheered and laughed the brothers worked in terrible silence. Mr Wilkens's face was bleeding, his clothes torn and his carefully combed hair completely dishevelled. Moena Mooies tried to intervene but was dragged screaming away by Mary. Finally the Jungle Boys were 15 done. Mr Wilkens was left lying semi-conscious next to his wrecked car.

The crowd slowly dispersed and walked back to their homes unwilling to be implicated as witnesses if the police arrived. The Jungle Boys dusted themselves, pulled their clothes straight and collected their 20 weapons. They returned to their home still in silence. They shooed their mother and sister in from the stoep, shut the door and drew the curtains. For a short time strains of jazz music filtered through into the street from their dining-room window. Then that stopped and the house lights were switched off one by one. 25

Jennifer

There was one fortnight in their lives that the inhabitants of Winsor Park would never forget. It was when Zoot fell hopelessly in love and as soon fell out of it again. It was the only time in his life that anything like that had happened, and afterwards when he thought about it he realised
30 how narrow a shave he had had. While the infatuation lasted, his relationship with The Boys became severely strained and the atmosphere in the house almost unbearable. To have a woman, and an upper-class woman at that, whom they had only seen on a photograph, come between them and Zoot seemed unbelievable. And to have it happen to
35 someone whom they respected as a leader, someone in whom they trusted …

It all started in a small way with the arrival of a letter inside a dainty blue envelope. It was addressed in a flowery handwriting to Mr Milton September, 203 Caledon Street. The postman knew no-one of that name
40 and, as he had never before delivered a letter to Winsor Park, had no idea where to put it. There was no letter-box. If Mr Punch Davids had had one it had long disappeared. If only the postman had had the sense to take it back to the dead-letter department he could have saved much unpleasantness. Instead he conscientiously pinned it prominently
45 against the pink door. There it remained for the day. The Boys speculated about it but left it alone. That night when Zoot returned he realised with a shock that it was for him.

He read it through and then summoned The Boys to the dining-room. This was unnecessary as they were already there, curious about
50 the contents of the letter. He read it to them. It came from Miss Jennifer Peters of 'Mavlen', Walmer Road, Woodstock. She had heard about Mr Milton September, the poet, from his aunt who taught with her. She

---

5 **gear into action**: start to do sth.   10 **toss sb./sth.**: throw sb./sth.
14 **dishevelled** [dɪˈʃevəld]: untidy   18 **disperse**: auseinander gehen
19 **implicated**: involved   30 **narrow shave**: lucky escape   **infatuation**:
blinding love   31 **severely strained**: under great pressure   32 **unbearable**:
unerträglich   37 **dainty**: zierlich   48 **summon sb.**: call sb. to come to you

believed that he had once been at the school and later returned for a short time as caretaker. So they had something in common. She took the Standard Six class for English and especially loved teaching poetry. It would be wonderful if they could meet a real poet, one who had attended their school. She looked forward to meeting him. Could he come to tea 5 at her home on Sunday at 4 p.m.? Only her mother and herself would be at home as her father usually went fishing. She hoped that somehow the letter would find him as his aunt had been a bit unsure about his exact address. She looked forward to their meeting.

There was an ominous silence after Zoot had finished. 10

Oubaas grinned foolishly and asked, 'Is she a white lady?'

'Don't be silly. How can she be a white lady if she teaches with my aunt?'

'Well then I'm sure she must be young and pretty.'

'I don't even know who she is. This is the first time I hear about 15 her.'

'What does your aunt say?'

'My aunt never mentioned her the last time I was there.'

Zoot omitted to mention that the last time he had visited his aunt was at least a decade before, and until the arrival of the letter he had 20 been unaware that she was still alive. Since the letter proved that she was, it was a mystery to him how she knew where he lived.

'This Miss Jennifer must have read some of your poems,' said Pretty-Boy. 'Your good aunt must have given her some of your poems to read. She must be very proud of her nephew.' 25

Zoot knew there could not be any truth in his comments. Where would his aunt have found any of his poems unless she retained those he wrote about the principal before he left the job? They would hardly be the types of poems his aunt and this Miss Jennifer would appreciate.

'I have always maintained that my friend Zoot is a famous writer. 30 Now we have this letter as proof of it. A lady who is educated and a school teacher from Walmer Estate invites him to have tea with her at her home. That is fame,' Pretty-Boy continued.

'I really wish I knew what my aunt could have told her to make her write such a letter.' He began to have serious reservations about his 35 aunt.

'You must find out for yourself. You must go and visit this learned lady and talk about your aunt and about your poetry.'

'I don't think I am up to that.'

40 'You must wear your check suit, comb your hair and then visit this lady.' Pretty-Boy insisted.

Oubaas grinned but it was uncertain whether he was agreeing or disagreeing.

'Hell, how does one behave when one has tea with a lady?'

45 'Perhaps Mary and The Girls will teach you how you must behave. Mary knows all about those things. Don't forget she is a priest's daughter,' Pretty-Boy added helpfully.

The next few afternoons when there were hardly any customers at the Casbah, Zoot rehearsed painstakingly in Mary's dining-room. He
50 was shown how to hold the cup so that his little finger pointed out stiffly. He was told how he must always leave a little tea at the bottom of the cup to show he was well-mannered and not greedy. He was instructed how to accept only one assorted biscuit at a time, place it delicately on a side-plate and then take dainty nibbles at it. He was admonished always
55 to refuse the second one. Zoot tried hard and was often on the verge of giving up.

He had his last rehearsal on the Sunday morning with The Butterfly standing in for Miss Jennifer Peters. That afternoon, in his check suit freshly pressed by Moena Mooies, wearing his Jarmans which still
60 contained the tap-dancing studs, he took the bus from Castle Bridge and walked up Walmer Road until he found 'Mavlen' on the upper left-hand side. It was a solidly built house with a neat garden and highly polished stoep. He opened the gate and walked up to the door, his studs clicking loudly on the cement pavings. He still had time to run away before
65 ringing the polished doorbell but what would they then think of him back in Caledon Street?

A young lady came to the door. She was pretty and fair-skinned and spoke English with a Walmer Estate accent.

---

35 **reservations** (pl): Vorbehalte   49 **painstaking**: very careful   54 **admonish sb.**: jdn. ermahnen   55 **on the verge of**: very near to

'You must be Mr Milton September. How wonderful of you to come. I'm Jennifer. Do you mind if I call you Milton? Do come in and make yourself at home.'

Zoot entered nervously.

'I'm so glad you've found the house. I know the name sounds absurd, but Ma's name is Mavis and Dad is Leonard, so it is called "Mavlen". There you have it.' 5

'It's a beautiful name,' Zoot said without conviction.

Mrs Peters made her appearance. She was huge and curt as her daughter was friendly. 10

'Ma, this is Mr Milton September, the poet I told you about. Milton, this is my mother.'

Zoot mumbled, 'Please to meet you,' as Mary had taught him to say.

Mrs Peters grunted some reply and turned to her daughter. 'So it's a poet this time. Last time it was that crazy violinist who played for the Spes Bona orchestra.' 15

'Oh Ma, don't give away all my secrets,' she said laughingly, then looked at Zoot. 'I heard a lot about you from your aunt. She really does admire your talent. I never told her I was going to write and invite you, so she doesn't know. Ma, Milton is the nephew of Miss September who teaches with me.' 20

Zoot managed to say that he had not seen his aunt very recently.

'And what sort of work do you do besides poetry, Mr September?' Mrs Peters barked.

'Who me? Oh, I'm in … how can I put it, I'm in business you might say. I work for a Miss Mary Brown whose father is a priest. I see to her security. You know what I mean.' 25

Mrs Peters made it clear that she did not know what he meant.

'Tea or coffee?' she asked abruptly.

'I beg yours?' 30

'Would you care for some tea or some coffee?' she repeated with exaggerated care.

'Some tea please if you don't mind.'

Mrs Peters went off to the kitchen.

'Don't bother about Ma. She's always like that. She bullies everyone, even me and Dad. Why do you think he's gone fishing today? Now you must forget her and tell me all about yourself.' 35

Zoot thought it best not to do so. Jennifer liked his reticence and put it down to modesty. She told him about her class at school, her interest in the arts, her love for painting, music and poetry, her regard for Byron.

'You mean my brother?' Zoot said surprised. His aunt must have been discussing the entire family with her.

'No, the poet.'

'Oh,' he laughed nervously, 'I thought you meant my brother Byron. I have not seen him for some time. I also have another brother called Keats.'

'How perfectly marvellous. So it runs in the family.'

Mrs Peters returned with the tea-tray, then excused herself and left abruptly to have her nap. It was obvious that she did not approve of Zoot.

Once she had left the atmosphere thawed rapidly.

'I have a guardian angel that has always whispered to me that one day I would meet a pretty girl who would also be very clever. Do you believe in guardian angels?'

She laughed and said she did.

'Is this you?' he pointed to a photograph standing on the piano.

'Yes. It was taken at the Arts Ball last year. My boy-friend at the time was a violinist.'

'It's beautiful.'

'Would you like it?'

'I would treasure it.'

She inscribed it 'To my friend Milton the poet, from Jennifer.'

Zoot was beside himself.

'I will write a poem for you. I will write one right here. Have you pencil and paper?'

She fetched some and he composed one for her and then an unflattering one about his aunt the way he remembered her. This

---

8 **conviction**: Überzeugung   38 **reticence**: not saying very much   52 **thaw**: (here) become less oppressive   64 **be beside yourself**: (here) be extremely happy

amused Jennifer. He was tempted to do one about her mother but thought it wise to desist at the juncture.

Late that afternoon Mrs Peters was woken from her nap by the noise coming from the living-room. She went to investigate and found Zoot trying to teach Jennifer to tap-dance. He left soon after, clutching the 5 photograph, but not before he had arranged that he would take her to the Funfair at the Early Morning Market, the following Saturday. He tactfully suggested that he would meet her at the Walmer Road bus-stop to avoid her mother.

Zoot tap-danced his way up Caledon Street flourishing the 10 photograph. The Girls came out to watch and The Boys stood on the stoep in a puzzled group. All then crowded into the dining-room of Winsor Park to hear Zoot's account of his visit. He was so excited that he became incoherent at times. Jennifer was the prettiest, beautifulest, most gorgeous girl in the whole world. The photograph was passed around to 15 prove it. Mrs Peters was clearly a monster but who cared, if she had a daughter like Jennifer?

Zoot was a changed man. He spent days on end in his bedroom with the door tightly shut. Very rarely did he turn up for work at Mary's and when he did he would not speak to anyone. He spent the time in his 20 room composing poems about Jennifer, for Jennifer, to Jennifer. He fixed the photograph above his bed and spent hours looking at it. He shifted the radiogram into his room and played over and over again a scratched recording of 'I Dream of Jeannie with the Light-brown Hair' until he drove The Boys crazy. He ignored them and kicked Oubaas twice 25 through sheer frustration. Oubaas simply grinned back at him. Life became very strained at Winsor Park and The Boys' happy-go-lucky, carefree lifestyle was seriously threatened.

That Saturday he met Jennifer by arrangement at the bus-stop. He had an exercise book full of poems for her as a present. By request Mary 30 had grudgingly advanced him extra money in addition to his weekly wages. He had never asked for extra money before.

Jennifer was in high spirits at the Funfair. They bought tickets at the coconut-shy. Zoot did a little tap-dance, wound his arms up, threw with deadly accuracy and won a teddy-bear which he presented to her with a 35 flourish. With Jennifer at his side he was a devil behind the wheel of the

Dodgem Cart and bumped everything in sight. They went on the swings and he placed her in the swing in front of his. He kicked, pushed and twisted hers until she screamed with fright. She then refused to
40 accompany him on the Big Wheel and, sulking, he climbed alone into the seat. As he was hoisted aloft he leaned forward recklessly to keep her in view and, when his seat was at the apex, he slipped and Jennifer gasped with horror when she saw the tiny figure suspended high above her hanging from the bottom bar of the seat. A crowd gathered as the
45 Big Wheel was turned slowly until a shaken Zoot was deposited on hard ground. There was relief and instantaneous applause all round. He did a tap-dance of victory and asked Jennifer right there in front of the crowd to become engaged to him. She said that she would consider it and let him have an answer.

50 When he returned home late that evening Zoot announced to The Boys that he had asked Miss Jennifer to become engaged to him. He was expecting her positive reply at any moment. He thanked them for their friendship over the years but unfortunately all that was now over. He would give them at most a week in which to find alternative
55 accommodation. Her mother might turn nasty and in that case Miss Jennifer might have to move into Winsor Park. There would obviously be no room for them as well as Jennifer and Zoot. A poet and his wife needed space and privacy. Zoot then returned to his bedroom, banging the door shut behind him. The scratched strains of 'I Dream of Jeannie
60 with Light-brown Hair' sifted through to the astonished boys.

Pretty-Boy was the first to recover. 'It is obvious that we are no longer good enough for Mr Zoot September,' he said bitterly. 'We were only good enough when we paid him his rent.'

'When was that?' Oubaas asked in astonishment.

---

2 **desist**: (von etwas) absehen   **juncture**: point in time   10 **flourish sth.** [ˈflʌrɪʃ]: wave sth. around   27 **strained**: not relaxed or friendly   **happy-go-lucky**: uncomplicated and easy   31 **grudging**: very reluctant   **advance sb. sth.**: pay sb. sth. before the work is done   34 **coconut-shy**: Wurfbude   35–36 **with a flourish**: schwungvoll   37 **dodgem cart** [ˈdɒdʒəm]: small electric car at a funfair   40 **sulk**: schmollen   41 **hoist sb./sth. aloft**: pull sb./sth. upwards   **reckless**: ignoring any danger   42 **apex** [ˈeɪpeks]: highest point   55 **turn nasty**: become unpleasant
59 **the scratched strains**: die kratzigen Klänge

'If we had the money we would have paid him his rent. We always meant to some day. That is the same thing. But now we are no longer good enough.'

'This is a sad day for us,' Boere said. He seldom spoke and the remaining two were amazed that he now ventured an opinion.   5

'And why is it a sad day?' Pretty-Boy asked, and when no-one replied he provided the answer. 'Because that Jezebel, that harlot has turned our friend's head. I wish her mother would force her not to marry our friend Zoot.'

'Maybe her mother should be persuaded that she should not marry   10
our friend Zoot. Maybe her mother should be given reasons,' Oubaas said and grinned stupidly.

Pretty-Boy was about to say something when he stared at Oubaas in amazement.

'You know, Oubaas, I think there are times when under your thick   15
skull I'll swear there is a genius.'

That Monday afternoon Pretty-Boy prevailed on Last-Knight to give him a haircut and shave on credit. He offered as repayment a week's supply of the best hair-restorer on the market, from a friend at bargain price. On the strength of that he also borrowed five shillings for the fare. He   20
dressed as best he could, adding Boere's tie and handkerchief which he had worn when first he came to the party at 203. Then he took the bus to Walmer Road.

After Zoot's rapturous description he soon found 'Mavlen'. Mrs Peters answered the door. Pretty-Boy had timed it so that Jennifer would still   25
be at school. However he did not expect Mrs Peters to look quite as fierce as she did.

'Excuse me, please, I am looking for Mrs Mavlen Peters.'

'I am Mrs Mavis Peters. Mavlen is the name of the house,' she said icily. 'What do you want?'

'I have come about Miss Jennifer and Mr Zoot September.'   30

'Who?'

'I mean Mr Milton September, you know, the poet.'

'Oh, that one? Can't say he is one of my favourites. I'm afraid Jennifer is still at school. Anyway it looks as if she is now in love with some painter or other.'   35

'I've not come to see her. I've come to see you. I'm Mr Milton's closest friend. We live in the same house. We are almost like brothers. My name is Mr Pretty-Boy Vermeulen.'

He opened his blue eyes wide and looked the picture of innocence.

40 'There are things about Mr Milton I think you must know. I came specially to tell you.'

'All right then, come inside,' she said reluctantly.

Pretty-Boy entered as ordered and sat gingerly on the edge of a chair.

45 'We heard he is going to get engaged to Miss Jennifer.'

'Over my dead body. And that goes for the new boy-friend as well.'

'That's why I came all the way to see you. It is to ask you to see that they don't become engaged, I don't really know how to begin.'

'What have you got to tell me?'

50 'As I said, why your daughter mustn't get engaged to Mr Milton.'

Mrs Peters was curious.

'Why mustn't my daughter get engaged to Mr Milton? Not that I don't agree with that.'

'You know he writes poems?'

55 'Yes, I believe so.'

'And tap-dances?'

'I have experienced it.'

'Those are usually the signs,'

'Signs of what?'

60 'They came on before his first wife disappeared.'

'What on earth are you talking about?'

'Why his first wife disappeared.' He stared innocently at her.

'You mean that while he was coming here to my daughter he was a married man?'

65 'That's not the worst of it. His first wife simply disappeared.'

'Why on earth did she disappear?'

'The way he treated her after he got those diseases.'

---

5 **venture an opinion**: say what you think   7 **Jezebel**: evil immoral woman
harlot: prostitute   7–8 **turn sb.'s head**: jdm. den Kopf verdrehen   16 **skull**:
Schädel   20 **on the strength of**: on the basis of   24 **rapturous**: enthusiastic

Pretty-Boy stretched his eyes wide. He was beginning to believe in what he was saying.

'I can't make any sense out of what you are saying. What diseases?'

'You mean you really don't know about his syphilis and that other thing – what do you call it again? – gonorr … something. You mean he never told you?'

'Good heavens. Of course not.'

'Before he gets his attacks there are signs. He writes poetry and he tap-dances.'

'What on earth are you talking about?'

'Then it goes to his head. He goes mad. He does terrible things. His first wife simply disappeared, Mrs Peters, I must please ask you to keep your daughter away from him. He can be very dangerous.' There were tears in his eyes.

'But surely his aunt would have known and warned Jennifer?'

'She's too ashamed of it. The family never mentions it. We don't mention it in the house in case it makes him worse. That's why his first wife simply disappeared with the children.'

'What children?'

Pretty-Boy realised that he was overplaying his hand.

'Never mind, Madam. I think you understand. I must go now. Milton was tap-dancing again this morning and I'm afraid he might be writing poetry right now. Please keep Jennifer away from him.'

Three days later a second letter arrived for Mr Milton September. This was from Mrs Mavis Peters and ordered him never to come to her house or see her daughter. She had received information about him from one of his friends, who seemed to behave like a lunatic. After she had spoken to her daughter they had mutually agreed that she would never see him again. She had another boy-friend, an artist who was a student at Michaelis. This correspondence was now at an end.

Zoot could make no sense of the letter and was tempted to go to Walmer Road and have it out with Jennifer and her mother. He spent the next few days in his room composing poems about the fickleness of women, especially those who had monsters for mothers.

Then one day he flung open his door and came out clutching 'I Dream of Jeannie with the Light-brown Hair' in one hand and Jennifer's

photograph in the other. He gave Oubaas a friendly kick and then did a
tap-dance on the back-porch. The Boys watched suspiciously.

40 'My guardian angel and I have had a long talk. It told me this morning
that I have been neglecting my good friends because an evil woman has
turned my head. I want my good friends to stay with me in my house
and pay my rent for ever. I must now ask my friends to make a small fire
so that we can sacrifice these worldly things.'

45 Oubaas and Boere gathered some sticks and newspapers and lit a
small fire. Zoot carefully placed the record and photograph on top of it.
As the flames began to lick he did a little tap-dance. The Boys showed
little emotion but there was relief in their eyes.

20 **overplay your hand**: go too far   27 **lunatic** (inml): mad person   28 **mutual**:
gegenseitig   33 **fickleness**: inconsistency   35 **fling sth. open** (**flung – flung**):
throw sth. open

Mrs Knight

Many in the congregation were sceptical about Mary's regular display of piety, genuine as it most probably was. She attended services dressed in sober black, took communion and put money in the offering-plate. Father Rowland however never doubted her sincerity. He came from England and had been parish priest in the District for more than ten years. If he was pleased to see Mary he never openly showed it, but then he never openly disapproved of her questionable profession either. He maintained a teasing relationship with Mary and The Girls.

But Mrs Joseph Knight made it very clear that she was unhappy about Mary's presence at services, even if she was her husband's former sister-in-law. And as wife of the chief churchwarden, she stated her views in no uncertain manner to whoever would listen or would be forced to listen. She felt strongly about having a 'house of ill fame' on their very doorstep, run by a relative, albeit by marriage, of her husband. No wonder Knight-Before-Last had run away. She had three growing daughters, Faith, Hope and Charity, and had made it clear that at no time were they to address that woman in that house as Aunt Mary. She was a disgrace to the Knights. Faith was eleven years old and already asking questions. She still remembered when Mary had boarded with them. She wanted to know why her mother disapproved of her aunt, whom she liked and admired.

One Sunday when Mary was sitting at the back of the church, ignoring glances Mrs Knight was throwing at her whenever she turned around from the front row, Father Rowland in his sermon appealed to the congregation for extra volunteers to offer to run stalls for the annual church bazaar. Everyone knew that the roof was leaking over the choir stalls and everyone, he continued, could see that the broken stained-glass windows needed repairing. There was only a month left before the bazaar, which was one of the biggest fund-raising efforts of the church. If anyone wished to assist by running a stall, they could hand in their names to the chief churchwarden, Mr Joseph Knight, either immediately after the service was over or later at his home, 209 Caledon Street.

Mary returned to the Casbah filled with righteousness and enthusiasm. On the way she stopped next door, at Winsor Park, to instruct Zoot and
35 The Boys to attend an inaugural fund-raising meeting in her lounge at 2 p.m. The Butterfly and the remaining girls were ordered not to allow in any more customers and to get rid of those still on the premises. The red light was temporarily switched off and the meeting began promptly on time.

40 Zoot, Pretty-Boy, Oubaas and Boere represented Winsor Park. Mary, The Butterfly, Fiela Vreters and Moena Mooies represented the Casbah. Mary, remembering procedure from her Brigade days, called the meeting to order and explained its business. She was unanimously elected Madam Chair and went to sit at the head of the table. Zoot because of
45 his literary ability was made secretary and given a new exercise book for the minutes. In a fit of optimistic speculation at the prospect of much money coming in, it was decided to have joint treasurers. The Butterfly and Pretty-Boy were elected. Mary and Zoot were secretly happy because it meant The Butterfly could keep an eye on Pretty-Boy, who was quick
50 with his hands and suffered from occasional lapses of conscience. Everyone else was elected to serve on the executive, so everyone was satisfied. Enthusiasm ran high and a formal motion was adopted to have a stall at the church bazaar for which money and goods would be solicited. The joint treasurers were immediately despatched to the chief
55 churchwarden to inform him of the resolution.

Their plans grew as their enthusiasm bubbled over. Zoot was elected to design and supervise the building of the stall. Since the theme of the bazaar was 'Countries of the World', they decided to call their stall 'In a Persian Market'. The Girls would serve behind the counter as harem

---

1 **congregation**: people attending a church service   2 **piety** ['paɪəti]: Frömmigkeit
3 **sober**: simple   **offering-plate**: plate on which money is collected in a church
8 **maintain sth.**: keep sth.   **tease sb.**: jdn. necken   12 **in no uncertain manner**:
very definitely   14 **albeit** [ɔːl'biːɪt]: (here) if only   24 **appeal to sb.**: an jdn.
appellieren   25 **stall**: Verkaufsstand   33 **righteousness** ['raɪtʃəsnəs]: a feeling that
you are good   35 **inaugural** [ɪ'nɔːgjʊrəl]: very first   43 **unanimous** [ju'nænɪməs]:
einstimmig   46 **minutes** (pl): written notes of decisions that were taken   47 **joint**:
gemeinsam; gleichberechtigt   50 **lapse of conscience**: Gewissenslücke   52 **adopt
a motion**: accept the idea   54 **solicit sth.**: ask for sth.   **despatch sb.**: send sb.

dancers and The Boys would act as guardian eunuchs. Zoot was also asked to supervise the joint treasurers in fund-raising. He and The Boys would get donations from local businesses while The Girls would publicise their stall among customers and neighbours. A collection box would also be placed strategically in the foyer of the Casbah and patrons would be blackmailed or pressed to give generously. Enthusiasm was now so high that at one stage Fiela Vreters and Moena Mooies were almost at each other's throats. Just then a dejected Butterfly and Pretty-Boy came to report back.

The delegation had not even been allowed across the threshold of 209. Faith, the eldest daughter, who was a pretty eleven-year-old, answered the door. She called her father, and while the joint treasurers were explaining the purpose of their visit, Mrs Knight pushed her husband and daughter aside, and, with Hope and Charity peeping from behind her skirts, gave them a tongue-lashing. The church could do without the likes of them and their Madam, Mary Brown. She refused to call her Mrs Mary Knight since people might think they were related. The Knights were decent, God-fearing people. Mary had a bloody cheek to take holy communion, never mind attempting to have a stall at a church bazaar. It was adding insult to arrant impertinence. Mary should spend her time more profitably searching for her former husband instead of leading astray many present husbands. Mr Joseph Knight was not well, and they should know better than to wake a hard-working man from his Sunday afternoon nap with an absurd request like theirs. Last-Knight had looked ashen even under his dark skin. Then the door was slammed ignominiously in their faces.

The meeting listened to the report in stunned silence. Zoot was the first to react. He suggested that he and The Boys, possibly assisted by The Jungles if necessary, should immediately visit the Knights and do some persuasion their own way. Mary, who had sat stone-faced, got up without a word and reached for her hat and coat. She left the house while the rest of the meeting crowded the doorway to watch the confrontation. But she passed by 209 without a glance at it and turned down Clifton Hill into the church vestry.

Father Rowland was busy preparing his sermon for evensong.

'If you can spare a moment, Father, may I speak to you please?'

'Of course. I can always spare a moment for you, Mary. You do look upset. Please sit down.'

'I am very upset, Father. You remember at the service this morning
40 you asked for volunteers to have stalls at the bazaar?'

'I certainly do remember.'

'Now me and The Girls were thinking, if our church needs help then we must help. Isn't that right, Father?'

'It is very kind of you.'

45 'So we decided with Zoot and The Boys to have a stall. "In a Persian Market" – that's what we meant to call it, Father.'

'What a splendid idea.'

'Unless you feel that it don't sound decent.'

'What could make you think so? I see absolutely nothing wrong with
50 it. In fact it sounds delightful to me.'

'Then you don't really mind, Father?'

'Of course I don't really mind.'

'About me and The Girls, I mean.'

'I feel honoured that you wish to help your church.'

55 'We tried to give our name in to Mr Knight, but his wife was very rude and would not accept it.'

'You must not mind Mr Knight. He is not a healthy man. He's been having a little trouble with his heart lately. Mrs Knight means well. However I shall speak to both of them and I'm sure it will be in order.
60 You go ahead with the Persian Market.'

'Then you don't mind, Father?'

'Of course I don't mind. And if Moena is going to bake the koeksisters for the stall I must place my order for a dozen right now because I know there will be a demand.'

65 'I will see that you get them. Thank you very much, Father.'

---

8 **dejected**: depressed   10 **threshold** ['θreʃhəʊld]: doorstep   16 **the likes of
sb.**: people like sb.   18 **bloody cheek**: unglaubliche Frechheit   20 **arrant
impertinence**: absolute Unverschämtheit   22 **lead sb. astray**: vom rechten
Weg abbringen   25 **ashen**: grey   26 **slam sth.**: throw sth. shut   **ignominious**
[ˌɪgnə'mɪnɪəs]: schmachvoll   27 **stunned**: shocked   35 **sermon**: Predigt
evensong: evening church service

'It is I must thank you. I look forward to your stall. Give my regards to Zoot and The Boys and my love to The Girls.' He winked an eye conspiratorially at her and proceeded with preparing his sermon.

The report-back meeting the following Sunday afternoon was a gloomy and depressing affair. The Boys had had no luck with local businesses, and not a single shopkeeper had been prepared to give a donation. In fact Katzen had reminded Zoot about the long outstanding rent for Winsor Park. Moodley, the Indian grocer, said business was bad enough without a bunch of no-good loafers trying to get donations. Mr Angelo Baptiste, the meek Italian general dealer whose dark shop off Seven Steps always smelt of onions and garlic, chased them away with a selection of choice Neapolitan epithets. The Girls had also had no luck either with neighbours or with customers. It seemed that Mrs Knight had made the rounds and blamed her husband's worsening health on the visit that The Butterfly and Pretty-Boy had paid them. And to think that in addition Father Rowland was allowing those no-goods to have a stall at a decent church bazaar …

The meeting sadly adopted a new resolution that although they would not give up the fight and would still have a stall, it would be a more modest affair than the one originally visualised. There would be no Persian Market. Moena Mooies would supervise the baking of koeksisters and the frying of samoosas, and the other girls would knit doilies when they were off duty. No customers had placed any money in the collection box, except a drunken Japanese seaman who thought it was an extra tax. The atmosphere had plunged to its lowest ebb when there was a knock at the door. The Butterfly was told by a despondent Mary to tell the would-be-customer to come back later in the afternoon when the red light would be switched on. She returned with little Faith Knight, who was crying bitterly.

Her father had taken a turn for the worse. It looked like his heart again. Her mother was beside herself. The children had not eaten all day and in desperation Faith had sought out her aunt. Mary listened in silence. She had not been in her brother-in-law's house for ten years. She stood up resolutely.

'I declare this meeting to stand adjourned until next time. Come, girls!'

They found a bewildered Mrs Knight sitting next to her husband in his unmade bed. She was ineffectually rubbing his hand while moaning incoherently. Hope and Charity were crying loudly in the kitchen. The
40 house was untidy and looked as if it had not been cleaned for days. Dirty plates and cutlery were piled high in the kitchen sink. Mary took immediate control. Zoot was sent to start the Knights' Studebaker and go to fetch Dr Cohen in Walmer Estate. Moena was told to go back to the Casbah to get food and clean linen. Fiela supervised The Boys in
45 cleaning the house. The Butterfly took charge of the children. Mary found hot water and a vinegar rag and started to swab Late-Knight's face. Mrs Knight was far too bewildered to offer any opposition even if she had wanted to, and sat whimpering in a corner. After an examination Dr Cohen said that there was no immediate cause for alarm but Mr
50 Knight should as soon as possible be placed under observation. It seemed that he had suffered a mild heart attack. The Boys carried him gently to the Studebaker and, with Zoot driving, Mary and Mrs Knight accompanied the sick man to Woodstock Hospital.

When they returned that evening with the news that the barber was
55 in no danger, comfortable and resting, the house was shining clean. There was a pleasant sound of soup bubbling appetisingly on the stove and The Butterfly was romping on the floor with Faith, Hope and Charity. Once the children had been put to bed, all the helpers left except Mary. Mrs Knight made a pot of tea and the two spent the evening
60 reminiscing about the time when Mary had boarded there and speculating what had happened to that no-good ex-husband of hers, Knight-Before-Last.

The response to Mary's bazaar appeal was still minimal. There was still a complete lack of any donations. Then Zoot reported that he had

---

3 **conspiratorial**: verschwörerisch   4 **gloomy**: dark   9 **bunch of no-good loafers**: group of useless, lazy, immoral people   12 **epithet**: curse   25 **plunge to its lowest ebb**: fall to its lowest point   26 **despondent**: depressed   32 **desperation**: state of having no hope   **seek sb. out (sought – sought)**: look for sb.   35 **adjourn sth.** [ə'dʒɜːn]: etwas vertagen   37 **bewildered** [bɪ'wɪldəd]: confused   38–39 **moan incoherently**: make sad noises   46 **swab sth.**: clean sth. with a cloth   48 **whimper**: wimmern   56 **bubble appetisingly**: appetitanregend brodeln   57 **romp**: jump around   60 **reminisce**: share memories   63 **appeal** (n): Appell

come home one evening to find an enormous box on his back porch. What was his surprise, he claimed, but to find it filled with plastic dolls. Katzen's name was partly erased from the lid. Whoever had left it must have intended it as a bazaar donation. What other use could they have for plastic dolls? So he took it to Mary who received it gratefully as a gift 5 from the unknown patron and put it into her back-room. Then Pretty-Boy was amazed to find two rolls of crêpe-de-chine just lying like that on their porch. Boere said that he found a dozen cartons of cigarettes (which looked as if they might have come from Moodley's shop) and Oubaas grinned and brought over a whole barrel of spaghetti with the 10 price marker of Angelo Baptiste still stuck in it. Mary's back-room started filling up as the anonymous donor or donors poured in gifts. The back porch of The Boys seemed to hold a curious attraction for whoever it was. The Boys found a large unopened crate of paper Italian flags, hessian bags of sourfigs, slabs of salted fish wrapped in waxpaper, 15 chinese lanterns and boxes of tinned meat. What was even more curious was that only The Boys seemed to make these discoveries. But then it was on their back porch that things were being left.

A week later a delegation of local shopkeepers demanded to see the committee. By this time dozens of bottles of cough mixture, parcels of 20 plastic combs and bouquets of paper flowers had found their way onto the porch. Katzen acted as spokesman for himself, Moodley and Angelo Baptiste. They wanted a truce. They were not accusing anyone of anything but they wanted a stop put to their goods disappearing. Sometimes goods went missing in broad daylight, under their very noses. 25

'Perhaps it is your guardian angel,' Zoot suggested. 'Perhaps it is because you are not a generous man. Perhaps if you helped us with the bazaar the angel might relent. Guardian angels like people who like church bazaars. They do not help people who are stingy.'

Katzen looked as if he was about to burst. Zoot continued innocently. 30 'One must never try to understand the ways of one's guardian angel. Perhaps if you gave a donation the angel might take pity.'

Angelo Baptiste was a quiet man unless aroused, when he would show his Latin temperament. He began speaking softly.

'A whole crate of Italian paper flags disappeared in broad daylight.' 35

'Perhaps it shows the love your guardian angel feels for Italy. You must have a Roman Catholic guardian angel that loves Italy.'

Angelo thought for a moment, looked hard at Zoot and capitulated. 'All right. I want peace. I will donate a dozen bottles of olive oil.'

40 'Your angel will feel happier if you also donated twenty pounds.'

'And twenty pounds.'

'And whatever paper flags are left.'

'How do you know there are any left?'

'My guardian angel suggested it to me.'

45 Moodley was also prepared to donate £20 and in addition all the rice and spices needed to make the breyani for the stall. Katzen attempted to show some fight and made references to the large amount of unpaid rent owing to him for Winsor Park. When Zoot quietly suggested that he could be disgracing his guardian angel with such stingy behaviour, he

50 grudgingly donated £20 and a dozen mounted and framed prints of King George VI and his queen.

Guardian angels of all nationalities and religions must have been satisfied for suddenly all thefts stopped and the back porch remained cluttered as it always was with weeds, rusty tins and empty bottles. One

55 outsider from Bo-Kaap tried to steal a carton of candles from Moodley and was caught by Pretty-Boy and Boere, given a hiding on the spot and sent packing back to Buitenkant Street.

The day of the bazaar was warm and pleasant. Zoot and The Boys had done a good job of the stall. There it stood, the 'Persian Market', splendid

60 with cardboard cut-outs of turrets and minarets, plastered all over with paper Italian flags. The dazzling creation stood out against drab stalls representing Brazil and Scotland, selling mundane items such as vegetables, pot-plants and back-numbers of *Readers Digest*. At both ends of the stalls The Boys mounted guard, wearing red fezzes, coloured

65 waistcoats and Turkish trousers. Behind the counter The Girls were ready to serve in turbans, revealing crêpe-de-chine blouses and billowing, almost transparent pantaloons. In the middle of them sat the

---

15 **slab**: flat piece   23 **truce**: agreement to stop fighting, etc.   28 **relent**: stop making trouble   29 **stingy**: not generous   33 **arouse**: provoke   46 **breyani**: rice dish   49 **disgrace sb.**: bring shame to sb.   60 **turret**: small tower   61 **drab**: grey and boring   62 **mundane**: uninteresting   65 **waistcoat**: Weste

Madam herself, resplendent in an enormous yellow turban studded with bits of coloured glass, and a huge, flowing red gown. For atmosphere The Butterfly played a scratched record of Ketelby's 'In a Persian Market' over and over again on a gramophone.

The stall had everything on sale from plastic dolls to dried fish, from noodles to prints of King George VI and his queen. But people were still unsure about buying there and passed by in order to purchase pot-plants at more mundane stalls. Then the Knights arrived. In front walked Faith, carrying a parcel tied with an enormous bow. Then came Hope and Charity holding hands and, bringing up the rear, Last-Knight, still ashen and frail, supported by his beaming wife. They stopped in front of the 'Persian market' and everyone at the bazaar stopped to watch. Faith gave a little bow and handed over the gift to Mary. There was an ominous silence in the hall. Only the scratched strains of Ketelby's music squeaked loudly. Mary undid the wrapping, raised the lid and revealed twelve bottles of the best hair shampoo. There was spontaneous applause all round. The Reverend Father Rowland, who had been watching closely, now walked over to purchase his dozen koeksisters. Mary on behalf of her stall committee presented him with a mounted and framed print of King George VI and his queen, and Fiela pinned a paper Italian flag to his lapel. After that the 'Persian Market' did a roaring trade and at one stage the hall looked as if it were celebrating Italy's national day.

When the Reverend Father made his speech at the close of the bazaar, the loudest applause came when he referred to the 'Persian Market' and thanked their committee. The Boys beamed and The Girls tried to look demure. Mary was all proud smiles.

'And I can say without the slightest hesitation', Father Rowland concluded, 'that when our need was greatest, when it was most pressing, it was Mary and her helpers whom we found the most willing and most obliging.'

---

1 **studded**: decorated with glass or metal   15 **reveal sth.**: uncover sth.   18 **on behalf of**: in the name of   21 **lapel** [lə'pel]: Revers

Part Two:

Afternoon 1960

Five years later, and a few years before the trickle of people leaving would become a flood. I remember the Big Days such as Christmas and New Year. But especially Christmas. Those were glad times and sad times before the official letters came in brown envelopes from the Board, before the inspectors
5 *came with their questions and forms, before the threats to be moved became real. The days before the minor diaspora. Those were the years when we believed that we in District Six would live there for ever, that if anyone moved it was because the rent had not been paid or the lights had been cut or they just felt like moving. Nobody ordered anyone else to move anywhere because of the*
10 *colour of their skins. Moving in our vocabulary meant going to live in the next block or the next street or maybe shifting from Clifton Hill to Horsburg Lane.*
We prepared for Christmas from the day or maybe the week before. Some say that people in the District prepared for Christmas from the Boxing Day before. I remember the air of expectation on Christmas Eve and then the
15 *reality of Christmas in District Six during the days before we were shifted to Hanover Park and Bonteheuwel and Manenberg. Sometimes today, especially during those Big Days, our eyes still travel over the mounds of rubble, beyond the man-made craters and the piles of dead soil to the celebration of Christmas past. We still remember.*
20 *My Christmas Day, when I was sweet fifteen and rapidly growing up, when I was at High School and wore long trousers for the first time, when I was in love and carefully cultivated my first moustache and practised making my voice deeper, always started the evening before. Elvis was king and we all wore curls on our forehead in imitation of Tony Curtis. As the first bells of St*
25 *Mark's rang out an hour before midnight, we began dressing in order to attend mass. I tried hard to feel grown-up but was already sleepy, and the tolling reverberated through my drowsy head. The dark had rolled down Table*

1 **trickle**: small flow   13 **Boxing Day**: the day after Christmas Day   14 **air of expectation**: Erwartungshaltung   17 **rubble**: Geröll   18 **piles of dead soil**: heaps of dead earth   24 **curls on the forehead**: Locken auf der Stirn   **Tony Curtis** (born 1925): US actor   26 **tolling** (n): ringing of bells   27 **reverberate**: echo   **drowsy**: sleepy

Mountain and covered the streets and lanes and stoeps and houses. There was also the smell of rain in the air. The second tolling, half an hour later, was the signal for lamps to be blown out or lights to be switched off and keys turned to lock houses, as we began to mince our holier-than-thou way up Caledon Street to the incense-warm stone church on windy Clifton Hill. We smelt of Waynick's 5 hire-purchase suits and pungent Christmas-present deodorants. My older brother also smelt of cigarette smoke, and my one unmarried sister of a sweet and sickly eau-de-cologne called 'Passion at Midnight'. We solemnly made our way up the street avoiding puddles and ignoring invectives hurled at us by less holy Christmas Eve drunks bent on disturbing the peace. 10

While dressing at home, my eldest brother and I had been alone in the boys' room. He winked an eye at me and slipped over half a glass of whisky. He said it was only once a year and after all I had just written the Junior Certificate examination. I downed it in one gulp and felt my insides set on fire. Once in church I felt dizzy and nauseous. The drowsy atmosphere, the thick 15 smell of incense, the roll of the organ music, all turned my stomach. Fortunately I was supported on either side by two grown-up brothers in their new, stiff, navy-blue suits. I was not able to listen to the long, soporific sermon but did pick up the preacher's references to the joy of Christmas. I realised that this was not intended for me. Half-dreaming I agonised about the wickedness of 20 boys of fifteen, still at school, who drank whisky and then had the audacity to attend a church service. My stomach gave an extra turn. I was afraid of getting sick right there over my brothers' new navy-blue suits and disgracing the family. When they went up to take Holy Communion I was too miserable and ill to accompany them. 25

By the end of the service I was recovering rapidly. When we came out into the night it had rained slightly and a playful wind was gusting and mercifully blew the last fumes of whisky out of my head. Fatigue was now rapidly setting in and I walked back almost asleep, hooked into the arm of my sister supporting me. I crept into bed and was soon astride my cowboy stallion riding the range. 30 It was springtime in the Rockies and my six-guns exploded between strums from my guitar. I was oblivious of the low hum of discussion around our dining-room table of my mother and sister, who were speaking in the kitchen while cooking, of the gossip about who was in church and who was not and why. 35

Christmas morning blazed bright and apricot yellow. The wind had dropped and the sun had chased the dark and drizzle back over Table

Mountain. The streets were still mirror-wet and the lamp-posts glistened proud and upright. Christmas Eve drunks were evaporating with the water puddles.

40   *But in our home the family slept on as if dead, their new clothes neat on hangers in wardrobes or suspended against doors. I was the only one awake, feeling wonderfully refreshed as I breathed in the cool, robust air.*

The blare of a Christmas choir band burst into the morning and I rushed onto the stoep to watch. It was the 'Young Stars of the East' who trumpeted
45   *and strummed 'Christians, Awake' as if they meant it. The bandsmen wore white panama hats, white flannels and bright-red blazers with formidable badges on the breast pockets. Two men, one of whom was Last-Knight, our barber, proudly bore the banner aloft depicting a nativity scene under an enormous Star of the East, which proclaimed for all the world to read that the*
50   *band was established in 1934 and had as its motto 'Per Ardua ad Astra', which made it seem like a local chapter of the Royal Air Force.*

Mr Joseph Knight, the barber's correct name, was very dark-skinned and soon after he moved into the District, received the nickname of Last-Knight. His elder and even darker brother, Henry, helped out in the shop when it was
55   *full of customers or Joseph was away from work. On one such occasion when his brother was ill, Henry was running the shop. Alfie du Plooy had not had a haircut for three months and resembled a very shaggy St Bernard dog. His mother, who had a reputation as a shrew, sent him to have his hair cut. Mr Henry Knight took one look at his shaggy mane and sent him home with the*
60   *cryptic message that if his mother thought that any decent barber would plough through that jungle of hair for one shilling, she had another guess coming. Mrs du Plooy marched on the shop with a howling Alfie in tow.*

---

4 **mince**: walk in small steps   **holier-than-thou**: selbstgerecht   5 **incense**: Weihrauch   6 **hire-purchase**: bought on credit   **pungent**: smelling strongly   8 **solemnly**: feierlich   9 **invective**: bad language   10 **bent on**: determined to   12 **wink**: zwinkern   15 **dizzy**: unable to balance   **nauseous**: sick   18 **soporific**: that makes sb. sleepy   21 **audacity**: nerve   27 **gust**: (of a strong wind) blow   28 **fatigue**: tiredness   30 **stallion**: male horse   32 **oblivious**: unaware   37 **drizzle**: light rain   43 **blare** (n): Plärren   47 **badge**: Abzeichen   48 **bear the banner aloft**: carry the banner high   50 **per ardua ad astra**: through hard work to the stars (motto of the RAF)   57 **shaggy**: with long untidy hair   58 **shrew** (infml): bad-tempered woman   61 **plough through sth.**: etwas durchpflügen   61–62 **have another guess coming**: have to think again   62 **in tow**: pulling behind

Arms akimbo she stood in the doorway and, not finding Last-Knight there as she had expected, addressed his brother.

'If you don't cut my boy's hair right now for one shilling, I'll hit you that you'll look the night before last.' The name stuck and the brothers were known from then onwards as Last-Knight and Knight-Before-Last. Now Last-Knight 5 proudly bore the banner of the 'Young Stars of the East' behind a much older and less hirsute Alfie du Plooy as drum-major.

My family had by now woken up. I wished my mother and sister a merry Christmas and then my brothers, who seemed to be anything but merry. They had started their celebration immediately after the church service and were 10 now suffering from massive hangovers. I cleaned my teeth and washed my arms and face in water my sister had warmed for me on the primus stove. When we were all ready we sat down to a breakfast of hot, egg-rich bread dotted with sesame seed which my mother could bake to perfection. These slices were smothered in thick layers of melting butter and slabs of sweetmilk 15 cheese. My brothers merely pecked at them.

Then the presents. We had no Christmas tree so the presents were stacked up on the sideboard. I gave my mother a string of imitation pearls I had spent weeks selecting and months saving up for. My sister received a bottle of pungent perfume (not 'Passion at Midnight'), and my brothers, deodorants. I always 20 gave my brothers deodorants, the same brand. Then I received my presents. My brothers, I think spitefully, also gave me deodorants, the same brand. The men in our family seemed obsessed with deodorants, and the air smelt sweet and sickly as we all tested ours. From aunts and uncles who believed in my scholastic potential, I received books about schoolboys in England, Tom Merry, 25 Bob Cherry and the Boys of Greyfriars, as well as Beano and Dandy annuals. And a pocket knife which sprouted a multiplicity of blades and gadgets with a multiplicity of uses, even one for taking stones out of horses' hooves, if only we in District Six had had horses with hooves out of which I could take stones. And from my sister, a new wallet containing a crispy new five-pound note. My 30 mother always gave me 'something useful that you can share with the family'. It could be a kettle or a wardrobe or a piece of linoleum. The family kept up the pretence for at least a few days and made a great play of saying in my presence, 'Boil some water in Richard's kettle,' or 'Hang it up in Richard's wardrobe,' or 'Doesn't Richard's lino match the curtains nicely?' 35

Then I carefully removed my new clothes from their hangers – the shirt, tie and suit, which was navy-blue. Maybe one could only get suits at Waynick's on

hire-purchase if one chose navy-blue. Maybe every clothes shop in the District
had a sale at the same time of navy-blue suits. I put on my new shoes, which
40 *were pinching, and feeling decidedly uncomfortable went out into the street to*
team up with Ronnie, Norman and Armien who were all wearing new navy-
blue suits. On our way to morning service we stopped at Moodley's shop,
which was open since he was not a Christian. Neither for that matter was
Armien but he was our friend and went wherever we went even though he was
45 *a Muslim.*

Moodley's shop was dark inside and smelt of curry-powder and turmeric.
At the entrance one negotiated hessian bags rolled down at the top and filled
to the brim with beans, peas and lentils. We fervently believed, and it formed
the basis for much discussion among ourselves, that in spite of his advanced
50 *age, and frail and desiccated appearance, he still had enough energy for his*
three wives, all of whom he had bought in India. Two of them we had never
seen and it was rumoured that he kept them in the storeroom at the back with
the masala. The third served behind the counter. She was a pale, ghostlike
creature with a dot painted on her forehead, her teeth stained brown from
55 *chewing betel. We could just make her out in the permanent twilight of the*
shop. In a fit of extravagance we bought twisty ice-creams, turkish delight and
blackballs that stained our mouths when we sucked them.

The crowded congregation at morning service was stiff and starched. We
sat stiff in our starched rows sucking discreetly and loosening the laces of our
60 *overtight shoes. Armien was with us. I usually sat in the front row, where I*
could see the porcelain effigies displaying the nativity scene. My mind would
wander back to the Christmas plays at primary school, where I was usually
cast as a sheep which shepherds watched. My sister and brothers had also in

---

1 **arms akimbo**: with your hands on your hips   7 **hirsute**: hairy   12 **primus**
stove: camping cooker   15 **smothered in thick layers**: in dicken Schichten
getränkt   16 **peck at sth.**: eat sth. as a bird does   22 **spiteful**: in revenge
23 **obsessed**: besessen   25 **scholastic potential**: academic talent   26 **annual**:
comic series that appear as books at Christmas time   27 **sprout sth.**: etwas
sprießen   **multiplicity**: large variety   **blades and gadgets**: Schnickschnack
40 **pinch**: (Schuhe) drücken   47 **negotiate sth.**: walk with difficulty past
sth.   **hessian**: Sackleinen   47–48 **filled to the brim**: absolutely full   48 **fervent**:
firm   50 **frail**: thin and weak   **desiccated**: dried out   53 **masala**: Indian spice
mixture   56–57 **turkish delight, blackballs**: types of sweet   58 **starched**:
gestärkt   61 **effigy**: figure

their time always been cast as sheep, and my mother had fatalistically accepted that with our limited acting ability she would always have to alter the sheep's costume for the new incumbent. Then after one glorious audition I broke with mediocrity and was promoted to being a shepherd watching his flocks by night. I watched either too enthusiastically or maybe too unenthu- 5 siastically, for the following year I was demoted to rejoin the flock. Fortunately my mother had kept the costume. Now at fifteen I was long past such childish things as nativity plays. When the collection plate came round I generously took sixpence out of my stiff new wallet and dropped it in loudly so that those around me could hear. 10

Then out into the sunlight to do the wishing rounds. First to wish my married sister and her husband in Bruce Street, where I received a present and cake and ginger-beer. Then to wish my aunt in Coronation Road, where I received a pound note and cake and ginger-beer. Then to wish my Standard Two teacher, with whom I still maintained contact, in Lavender Hill, where I 15 received cake and ginger-beer. And then, because I could not face another slice of cake or glass of ginger-beer, I went home to the midday meal for which by now I had no appetite.

Everyone enjoyed the feast except me. The whole family was present. We wore paper caps and looked silly. We pulled paper crackers and looked even 20 sillier. We found cheap trinkets inside them and pretended they were pieces of treasure. We read the platitudes on the strips of paper in the crackers and discussed them as gems of wisdom. Then, with the sun shining warm outside, we started with hot, mutton curry, then the pièce-de-résistance, a huge, roast leg of lamb done to a turn, crunchy sweet potatoes, green peas and yellow rice 25 with raisins and cinnamon. Over the meat we poured thick, spicy gravy. Then, exhausted with eating and the heat, we still had a choice of fruit salad which we called 'angels food', rice pudding and trifle. The adults had wine and spirits with their meals and although I was offered a glass I wisely declined.

While the grown-ups took an afternoon nap, Ronnie, Norman, Armien 30 and I decided to take a joy-ride by train to Kalk Bay and back. We walked down empty streets to the semi-deserted station. Everyone seemed to be sleeping off heavy Christmas lunches. Although we bought first-class tickets (we had so much money) we still had to occupy coaches set apart for 'non-whites'. The sheer exuberance of speed as we flashed and rattled past houses, 35 trees and stations like Harfield, Wittebome and Retreat. The surly white conductor resented our shouting and laughing. Maybe he resented having to

work on Christmas Day. Glaring at us he demanded our tickets as if he hoped
to catch us out. I slowly drew my new wallet out of the jacket pocket of my new
40 *suit and extracted the ticket, which I presented with studied sang froid.*

We took off our shoes and socks, rolled up our trousers and walked along
the dirty beach. Even the sand had long given up being white and was now a
dirty grey. The beach was almost deserted, waiting for the hordes that would
descend upon it on Boxing Day. A few families were camping under blankets
45 *which acted as make-shift tents. Others sat under the arches over which the*
train rattled on its way to Simonstown. Some people were lying in the sun
eating watermelon. A few men sat in the shade drinking wine. Two were
already so drunk that they were gambolling in the dirty green water fully
clothed.

50 *By the time we returned home it was getting dark. Christmas bands were*
marching along the streets playing spirited hymns and carols. Older people
came out of their houses to sit on benches, gossip of just sit the evening away.
From a high stoep we ogled girls on the opposite stoep, who pretended to ignore
us.

55 *Ronnie produced a silver case filled with cigarettes and at a signal we all*
strolled nonchalantly to the field behind the church, where, out of sight, we lit
up, drew the blue smoke into our lungs, coughed and felt bilious. We smoked
until our heads were turning, lighting one cigarette from another. Then we
returned to the stoep feeling grown-up and sick.

60 *Dusk changed to dark, and dark was accompanied by the quiet of*
exhaustion. District Six rested from the hurry and bustle of yet another
Christmas. Here and there the sounds of a band still wafted faintly on the tired

---

3 **incumbent**: (here) owner **audition**: Vorsprechen 5 **flock**: Herde 6 **demote**
sb.: give sb. a lower position 13 **ginger-beer**: lemonade made with ginger
20 **cracker**: Knallbonbon 21 **trinket**: cheap jewellery 23 **gem of wisdom**: Perle
der Weisheit 24 **mutton**: meat of a male sheep **pièce-de-résistance**: masterpiece
26 **spicy**: würzige **gravy**: Bratensauce 28 **trifle** ['traɪfəl]: sweet dessert
29 **decline sth.**: refuse to have sth. 35 **sheer exuberance**: überschwengliche
Freude 36 **surly**: sauertöpfisch 37 **resent sth.**: strongly dislike sth. 38 **glare at**
sb.: look at sb. angrily 40 **studied sang-froid**: calculated coolness 45 **make-**
shift: notdürftig 48 **gambol**: jump around 51 **carol**: Christmas song 53 **ogle**
sb. ['əʊgəl]: stare at sb. 56 **nonchalant**: unbekümmert 57 **bilious**: sick
61 **hurry and bustle**: busyness 62 **waft faintly**: flüchtig wehen

*night air. Somewhere Bing Crosby was singing 'I'm Dreaming of a White
Christmas'. Many of the older people were happy that one of the Big Days was
over. Now only Boxing Day and New Year remained. Others were too tired to
care and just went on sitting breathing in the mountain air, fanning themselves
and speculating softly about how many more Christmases they would be* 5
*allowed to remain in District Six before someone in Pretoria ordered them to
move.*

I still clearly remember the characters and the incidents.

Knight-Before-Last

One day Mary received a very peculiar invitation. It was delivered at her
10 door by little Charity Knight. Inside a pink envelope was a card which
requested the pleasure of the company of Mrs Mary at a religious house-
meeting to be held at 209 Caledon Street, the residence of Mr and Mrs
Joseph Knight, at 4 p.m. that Sunday. It would be addressed by the
Right Reverend the Bishop of the Episcopal Church of God (Fordsburg,
15 Johannesburg). Tea would be served and a silver collection taken.
Normally Mary would have ignored such an invitation if she had ever
received one, but she considered this to be a peace-making gesture from
Mrs Knight. What caught her eye was that below the printed invitation
was a message in Mrs Knight's handwriting, 'Please come, Mary. The
20 bishop wishes to renew acquaintance – so don't disappoint.' Mary knew
one or two priests, after all her father was one, but she certainly knew
no-one as exalted as a bishop. How then could he wish to renew her
acquaintance?
    At the last minute Mary decided to go out of curiosity. Outside 209
25 she spotted a slick, shiny black Dodge bearing a Johannesburg
registration. Inside the house a few old, bored and uncomfortable people
sat on chairs against the wall. Mrs Knight, smiling broadly, came to meet
her at the door and introduced her to the special guest, who rose
majestically from his chair at the head of the table, his arms outstretched.
30 He looked dapper in purple and black and wore a large silver pectoral
cross around his neck. He was extremely dark of complexion, with
heavily plastered straightened hair. He also sported a thin Errol Flynn
moustache. There was something familiar about him.
    'Mrs Mary Knight, I presume?' he said arching his left eyebrow
35 teasingly.
    Nobody had addressed her as such for a very long time.

14 **Reverend**: title of a priest   20 **renew acquaintance**: meet again   22 **as exalted
as**: (here) in as high a position as   25 **Dodge**: brand name of a car   30 **dapper**:
well-dressed   30–31 **pectoral cross**: cross hanging over the chest   32 **Errol Flynn**:
US film actor

'Good gracious!' she said as memories flooded back, 'if it isn't Knight-Before-Last, I mean, Henry!'

'Yes, Mrs Knight, your long-lost husband Henry.'

They had parted very many years before. There had never been a divorce because Knight-Before-Last had been nowhere to be found. He had simply disappeared without a trace.

'Where on earth do you come from?' Mary asked astonished.

'Johannesburg, all the way from Fordsburg, Johannesburg through the mercy of the Lord, in order to save souls for Him in the Cape.'

'But what have you been doing all these years since you went away?'

'It's a long story, Mary. When I first came to Johannesburg I lived in the very pits of hell. I was a sinner, a miserable sinner. I sinned morning, noon and night. Then one day, while I was in a brothel, I had a vision. Yes, Mary, I had a vision right in a place as evil as all that.'

Mary felt distinctly uncomfortable.

'And then I heard a voice speaking to me. It said that I was chosen to establish the true church in order to preach the true gospel. That was more than sixteen years ago. I then became founder and first pastor of the 'King George VI, Win the War Hallelujah, Episcopal Church of God'. Now I am its bishop and head and have six congregations in Fordsburg and Coronationville and fourteen more scattered throughout the black townships. I am in Cape Town for a few days to spread the word and also to have a happy reunion with my brother, his family and my dear wife,' he looked at her coyly, 'whom I have neglected all these years.'

His brother was sitting in a corner with a sneer on his face. Last-Knight got up at the end of the bishop's explanation, mumbled something which sounded like 'Bullshit!' and left the room banging the door behind him. Mrs Knight looked embarrassed but the bishop seemed unperturbed.

'Mary, today I am more interested in your soul than in your body. That's why I wanted so desperately to meet you.'

He then preached to those present maintaining that they were destined for hellfire and damnation unless they became paid up members of the 'King George VI, Win the War Hallelujah, Episcopal Church of God'. There were tears in Mary's eyes by the time he had finished. She was so proud of him and so ashamed of her own wicked

way of life. It seemed she was destined to be associated with clergymen
of all ranks, even bishops.

40 Henry invited Mary to accompany him that very evening to a house-
meeting in Bishop Lavis township, where he was starting a new branch
of his church. She consented immediately. When he picked her up
outside the Casbah, she was wearing sober black, had removed all traces
of make-up, and was fiercely clutching a hymnbook and bible.

45 On the way back she confessed to him about the nature of her
business. He appeared to be shocked (although he had heard about it
the day before from his sister-in-law) and said he was impressed with
her honesty and was glad that he had arrived just in time to save her
soul from further damage.

The following afternoon Mary called a meeting of The Girls to meet
50 the bishop. She introduced him and he opened proceedings with a
prayer during which he launched scathing personal attacks on all those
present. Mary had confessed everything. He pleaded that the Casbah be
closed forthwith. Mary decided immediately that all activities would be
suspended until further notice. For the first time in its history the red
55 bulb was switched off indefinitely. The Girls spent the next few days
turning away angry customers while their Madam was away attending
house-meetings all over the locations and townships.

One evening The Butterfly invited all the Winsor Park boys over for
coffee and drinks. Everyone sat in a deep gloom and felt Mary's absence.
60 She was in Elsies River with Bishop Knight.

'That it should end like this,' Moena Mooies said.

'The end of beautiful friendships,' added The Butterfly sadly.

'That it should happen to our Mary of all people. To become
converted at her age,' Fiela Vreters commiserated.

65 'Maybe it's because her father's a priest. Such things run in families,'
Oubaas said and grinned stupidly.

---

12 **pits of hell**: Gräben der Hölle   17 **gospel**: Evangelium   25 **sneer**: höhnisches
Lächeln   33 **destined for hellfire and damnation**: going to hell   36 **wicked**:
evil; immoral   41 **consent**: agree   51 **scathing** (adj): bissig, scharf   52 **plead**:
inständig bitten   53 **forthwith** (fml): immediately

'The way I feel I can just pack up and we can all go quietly,' The Butterfly said fatalistically.

'Where to?'

'Where we came from originally. Wherever that is.'

They sipped their coffee in deep depression.   5

'If only we can find out something we can use against the bishop,' Oubaas suggested.

'Like what?' Pretty-Boy asked.

'Oh anything. I don't know. Anything we can use against him. He can't be perfect. Something to force Mary to leave him, and force him to   10
leave her.'

'Nonsense.'

'Maybe the Knights know something about him. I don't really know,' he said shrugging his shoulders.

Pretty-Boy looked up slowly.   15

'You know, Oubaas, underneath that thick skull of yours I think there is a genius struggling to get out.'

'I was only suggesting,' he said stupidly. 'If only there was something.'

'If only,' Zoot repeated. There was a strange look in his eyes.   20

Zoot strolled into Last-Knight's shop. The barber was finishing a customer in the chair, otherwise the place was empty.

'Good afternoon, my worthy tonsorial friend,' Zoot said seating himself and picking up a dated copy of *Drum*.

'To what do I owe the honour?' the barber asked suspiciously.   25

'My guardian angel suggested it was time I had a haircut and shave and maybe a bit of conversation.'

'What do you mean?'

'My guardian angel? But maybe barbers do not have guardian angels.'

'Are you prepared to pay?'   30

'Now, now, Mr Knight. Why so mercenary? Where's your Christian charity? Of course I'll pay once I have found an alternative source of income. I am about to lose my present one. The Casbah is closing down.'

'The bishop?' Last-Knight asked meaningfully.   35

'Yes, the bishop,' Zoot assured him.

'He might be a blood brother of mine but he is more a bloody hypocrite!'

'Really?' Zoot asked looking surprised.

40 Last-Knight brushed down the customer.

'Next!'

Zoot looked around at the empty shop. 'Who me?'

'Yes, you. I thought you wanted a haircut and a shave.'

'And maybe a bit of conversation and a bit of information about 45 bishops.'

'Then get on.'

Zoot climbed into the chair.

'If only Mary knew what we know about that bloody bogus bishop,' Last-Knight said acidly.

50 'What do you know about him, my tonsorial friend?'

When Last-Knight had finished he whipped the cloth from around Zoot's neck, winked an eye and said, 'Now my friend, you are not only road-worthy but also well informed.'

Zoot's hair was brushed flat and gleaming, his chin felt soft without 55 its normal stubble and he did a little tap-dance as he entered the Casbah. He pecked The Butterfly lightly on her check and said, 'You must now prevail on Mary to have a little farewell prayer-meeting. It could also serve as a time for the confession of sins. Friday afternoon seems suitable. Ask her to invite everyone in Buckingham Palace. Me and the 60 Boys will definitely be present.'

Mary was very happy to arrange the Friday meeting. It would be used to announce the transition of the Casbah from its normal use to a chapel of Bishop Knight's Episcopal Church of God. Everyone on the row was invited. The Abrahamses politely refused on religious grounds and Last-65 Knight repeated the single epithet 'Bullshit!', only louder and more

---

23 **tonsorial**: concerning hair   31 **mercenary**: over-interested in money
38 **hypocrite**: Heuchler/in   48 **bogus**: false   49 **acidly**: sharply   53 **road-worthy**: in a condition to be driven   54 **gleam**: shine brightly   55 **stubble**: Stoppel

distinctly than before. His wife, speaking on behalf of herself and her three daughters said that they would be delighted to attend.

Everyone crowded into Mary's dining-room. She sat proudly at the head of the table next to the bishop himself, who was resplendent in purple and black, playing with his silver pectoral cross. He started with a very long rambling prayer larded with obvious hints directed at those present. He prayed about the Casbah as a house of sin, about women who gave their bodies to men, about men who never worked but lived off others, of others like a close relative of his who didn't have the decency to wish to hear the word of God. He became more and more heated, encouraged by loud sighs and amens from Mary and Mrs Knight. Zoot listened quietly. At last the harangue was over and the bishop asked if anyone present had any doubts or wished to make a public confession. Oubaas was about to volunteer and was already on his feet when Zoot pulled him down.

'Your Eminence,' he started, 'I have some doubts. There are problems for which I have been unable to find any solutions.'

'Do not be afraid to speak to me, my child.'

Zoot had been called many things in his adult life but never 'my child'. Nevertheless he allowed this to pass without comment.

'Your Holiness, do you believe in the power of guardian angels?'

'Yes, I suppose I do.'

'I have a guardian angel that often speaks to me. You believe of course that guardian angels can speak to one?'

'Yes, I do. I also once heard a voice speaking to me in a house as sinful as this. It was in a brothel in Kliptown, Johannesburg.'

'My guardian angel says that a man must have only one wife. You agree with that?'

'What are you getting at?'

'You agree with it?'

'Yes, I agree with it.'

'Only one married wife?'

The bishop began looking uneasy.

'And if he has more than one married wife, he is guilty of – what's the word again?'

'Bigamy,' Pretty-Boy said.

'Yes, bigamy. It is not only against God's law but against man's law.'

The bishop waited for Zoot to continue.

'And my guardian angel also says that what could make it worse is if a man has children from the second wife. They are then called – what's the word again?'

'Bastards,' said Pretty-Boy.

'I'm not sure what you are getting at,' Bishop Knight said nervously.

'I believe it's even worse if those children happen to be two boys and a girl who are fourteen, twelve and eleven years old. My guardian angel is very precise about ages.'

'I wish you would come to the point,' the bishop said acidly.

'My angel says that it is bad enough if an ordinary man commits – what's it called again? – bigamy. And has three – what's its name? – bastards. But it's worse if someone important like a cardinal or a pope commits it, wouldn't you agree?'

'Maybe and maybe not.' The bishop cut him short. 'Is there anyone else who has any questions of wishes to confess? I haven't much time.'

'I'm a bit disappointed that you are not interested in what my guardian angel has to say. Mine is very knowledgeable especially about the ways of the clergy.'

Bishop Knight closed the service and angrily hurried out.

Charity Knight brought a letter to Mary the following morning. The bishop unfortunately had had to leave for Johannesburg at once. One of his pastors had suddenly become very ill and was now under intensive care. The bishop was rushing to be at his bedside. He would not be able to continue his mission in Cape Town for a long time and suggested that Mary should not follow him to Johannesburg as that place was even more sinful than Cape Town. He would never forget her and would keep her constantly in his prayers. He signed the letter, 'Henry Fordsburg.'

It took some time for Mary to recover but she did eventually and gradually reverted to her own ebullient self. She felt bitter about the way, twice now, Knight-Before-Last had run away from her.

---

6 **rambling** (adj): unstructured   **larded with**: full of   10 **decency**: good manners
12 **harangue**: Tirade   48 **commit sth.**: etwas begehen   56 **the ways**: the manner
in which sb. lives   **the clergy**: priests and ministers of religion   67 **ebullient**:
confident and full of energy

A week later Zoot sauntered back into the barber shop.

'You are not coming for another haircut and shave, I hope,' Last-Knight said.

'Not unless you insist. I have merely come to tell you that my guardian angel seems to think that bishops do not like to be asked 5 questions.'

'Maybe that is so,' Last-Knight sighed meaningfully. 'There are bishops and bishops. The self-appointed ones are also the self-opinionated ones. Those are the ones who do not like questions.'

'Since it is likely that barbers might not have guardian angels, you 10 know, to look after razors and brushes and hair-oil and confidential information, my angel has asked me to thank you personally.'

'For what?' Last-Knight asked.

'It doesn't really matter, does it? With a clean-shaven soul like yours my guardian angel would be proud to be associated. Thank you, once 15 again.'

He sauntered out to go and chat to Mary and The Girls at the Casbah.

Moena Lelik

Except for unexpected emergencies there was only one time during the
20 year when 201 was completely closed for business the entire day and
that was at New Year, when Buckingham Palace as a group went on its
annual picnic to Kalk Bay. This year the Knights would not be
accompanying them since they had been invited to spend the day with
relatives in Retreat.

25   Mary and Mrs Abrahams were in charge of the food. Helped by The
Girls and Moena Lelik, they baked, roasted and fried and what they still
needed they bought at Moodley's and Wellington's in town. The Boys
were in charge of drinks. They had salvaged what they could and Pretty-
Boy got the rest from his bargain-price friend. The Butterfly's old
30 gramophone had long ago been replaced with an expensive portable
radio and tape-recorder brought for her from Hong Kong by a Chinese
admirer.

The sun rose ripe and rich on New Year's morning. There was an air
of expectancy and well-being in the streets now dappled with light. The
35 dirt and sordidness had evaporated, leaving in their place a feeling of
warmth and cheerfulness. Across streets was strung thin cord to which
were tied bits of ribbon sporting the colours of local coon troupes. A
Hollandse team, the Young Coronations, came swaying down Tennant
Street, the members splendid in new outfits, tapping their canes
40 rhythmically on the asphalt in time to the music from their band. Other
coons were on their way to assembly points at club-houses, some already
in carnival dress but without make-up, others already in make-up but
without carnival dress. A festival atmosphere hung over the District,
waiting to explode into a rainbow of colour when the coons would make
45 their way to Hartleyvale and Green Point Track.

1 **saunter**: walk in a self-confident manner   8 **self-appointed**: selbsternannt
8–9 **self-opinionated**: eingebildet   28 **salvage sth.**: save sth.   34 **dappled**:
marked with spots of sth.   35 **sordidness**: quality of being poor and unpleasant
evaporate: verdunsten   37 **ribbon**: coloured band usu. for the hair   **coon troupe**:
group of singers and musicians who wear make-up and dress in unusual costumes

The picnic party met outside the Casbah. The Girls wore blouses, shorts, sandals and sun-glasses. Zoot and The Boys sported coloured, tropical shirts procured for them by Pretty-Boy. The Abrahamses arrived out of breath, having left Mr Abrahams at home where he preferred to stay with his newspaper and the radiogram on which he was going to   5
listen to the cricket at Newlands. Moena Lelik chatted excitedly to her cousin, with whom the family were now reconciled. The Jungle Boys helped with the packing. Laughing and joking, with The Butterfly's portable playing loudly, they took up baskets or carrier bags or blankets and made their way down past Castle Bridge to the already crowded   10
station. Mary generously paid for everyone, and the party squeezed into the third-class compartment. On New Year's Day everyone who was anyone from the District travelled third-class, which was already packed with families all going to Kalk Bay. The white ticket examiner blew his whistle stridently, then jumped into their coach at Mowbray. He started   15
pushing and shouting at the passengers. There was a minor scuffle, in the course of which his clippers were ripped from his hand. He hurriedly alighted at Rosebank, and the clippers came sailing out of a window, narrowly missing his head. For the rest of the journey he confined himself to the second- and first-class compartments and only re-entered   20
the third-class after Kalk Bay.

Almost the entire coach spilled out there and people rushed onto the beach to claim the best spots. Zoot and Pretty-Boy sprinted ahead and found a pleasant one near the arches. Then The Girls and Moena Lelik came up, followed by the rest in high spirits. The Jungle Boys began   25
making a rough shelter out of the blankets for protection against the sun which threatened to beat down fiercely later in the day. The Moravian Brass Band struck up from the playing-stand and the beach became more and more packed as train after train pulled in. The Girls frolicked in the water and teased Mrs Abrahams, Mary and Moena Lelik into   30
joining them. Then they rubbed themselves with suntan lotion and lay frying on the rocks while listening to music on The Butterfly's tape-recorder. Moena Lelik was far too shy to join in but waded in the shallows up to her ankles and screamed with delight when a roller broke at her feet. Pretty-Boy joined her, laughing and encouraging. While food   35
was being prepared the Jungle Boys went fishing at the end of the

wooden jetty with lengths of nylon and fierce-looking hooks. Zoot, Boere and Oubaas sat drinking under the railway arches.

It was decided that before lunch all would go on the boat-trip round
40 the bay – all, that is, except the Jungle Boys, who were fishing earnestly. The women shouted nervously when it looked as if the boat, packed with holiday-makers, was heading for the open sea. Moena Lelik was getting sick and Pretty-Boy placed his arms gently around her and spoke encouraging words.

45 A pleasant relationship seemed to be developing between the two. He was kind and solicitous and she was totally infatuated with this attention, but dared not think that he might really care for her. Pretty-Boy was genuinely concerned about this plain, lonely girl and felt protective towards her. At home he had always ignored her, with the
50 confidence of a man who could afford to ignore any woman because he was aware of his own obvious attractions. Now he joked with her, teased her about being a bad sailor, and offered her bits of food from his plate. Whenever he turned his blue eyes on her she shivered with a mixture of uncertainty and delight.

55 He was going to swim off the fishing-boat jetty and asked her to accompany him. As a youth he had learnt to swim like a fish in the reformatory swimming-pool. Now he dived into the deep, oily water between the boats. He jack-knifed and somersaulted and did tricks in the air that took away Moena's breath and had spectators cheering. His
60 body was smooth and muscular and bronze with sun-tan lotion The Girls had smeared on him. He crawl-stroked to the opposite jetty where her brothers were fishing and then swam back again. People queueing to go on a boat-trip cheered the unexpected display. Pretty-Boy was

---

7 **be reconciled**: be friends again   9 **portable**: (here) portable radio or tape player   **blanket**: Decke   15 **strident** ['straɪdənt]: shrill   16 **scuffle**: minor fight   17 **clippers** (pl): tool for stamping tickets   18 **alight** (v): get out (of a train)   26 **rough shelter**: simple structure   27 **fierce**: strong   28 **strike up** (**struck – struck**): start to play   29 **frolic**: play around   34 **shallows** (pl): area of water which is not deep   37 **jetty**: wooden platform that is built above water 46 **solicitous**: wanting to please   **infatuated**: fascinated   53 **shiver**: zittern 58 **jack-knife**: dive by folding your body together and then opening out **somersault**: roll over like a ball

enjoying the attention, and Moena Lelik was overwhelmed that this god
should be doing all this just for her.

After lunch the Jungle Boys went back to their unsuccessful fishing
and everyone else relaxed on the sand or rocks. Pretty-Boy suggested to
Moena Lelik that they could go for a stroll along the beaches to St James.   5
As they walked he told her about Johannesburg, how he learnt to swim
and when he had first met Zoot. She in turn told him that she had never
dared to tell how much she admired him. Her parents and brothers
loved her as she loved them, but they were far too protective towards
her. The two stood and held hands on the edge of the almost deserted   10
tidal pool at Dalebrook, watching the few children cavorting in the
water. Pretty-Boy held her tightly. Moena was blissfully happy.

A young white beach constable hurried towards them waving his
arms.

'Come on, come on, get off this beach. You're not allowed here!'   15
'Why not?' Pretty-Boy asked, annoyed at the uncalled-for hostility.
'Can't you read the notices? This beach is for white people only.'
'We're not making any trouble. We're just looking,' Moena said.
'Well you've looked enough. Now clear off the beach.'
'You don't speak to any lady like that,' Pretty-Boy said angrily.   20
'Let's go,' Moena pleaded. 'We don't want any trouble.'

'There will be plenty of trouble if you don't move fast. Want me to
fetch a railway policeman from the station?'

'You may do what you please. We'll move when we are ready.' Pretty-
Boy said evenly. 'And we are not ready yet.'   25

'If that's the way you want it, then you can have it.' The beach
constable hurried back through the subway.

'Let's go,' Moena said nervously.

'Don't worry about him,' Pretty-Boy reassured her. 'He's just bluffing.
All whites bluff all the time. That's most probably the last we'll see of   30
him.'

They started walking back towards Kalk Bay. The beach constable
came running after them with a bored railway police sergeant in tow.
Pretty-Boy did not quicken his pace although Moena nervously gripped
his hand.   35

'Hey you, you there, stop where you are,' the beach constable
shouted.

They went on walking at the same pace, ignoring the shouts.

'Can't you hear me? I said, stop there!'

40 Pretty-Boy and Moena waited until they came up.

'These are the two, sergeant.'

The railway policeman was obviously more annoyed with the beach constable than with them.

'You know you're on the wrong beach?' he said, going through the
45 motions.

'I wasn't aware of it,' Pretty-Boy said.

'Well, you are now, and you are breaking the law. I can arrest you and that's not a pleasant way to start the new year, is it?'

'You must do what you mean to do,' Pretty-Boy answered flatly.

50 'I don't understand you people. You have your own beaches. Why must you come here to swim? White people don't go to your part.'

'We were not going to swim. We were just walking across this section on our way to St James.'

'Please, sir,' Moena was now near to tears. 'We don't want any trouble.
55 We are leaving now.'

'O.K. I'll let you off this time, but don't let me catch you here again. Stay on your own beach or, if you want to walk to St James, then take the Main Road.'

Pretty-Boy said nothing but there was a hostility in his blue eyes that
60 was ugly and frightening.

'Come,' he said fiercely to Moena. They continued walking to Kalk Bay in silence.

Pretty-Boy would not speak about the incident but Moena burst into tears when she saw her mother, and blurted out the full story. The Jungle
65 Boys were fetched and were all for sorting out the beach constable immediately. Their mother dissuaded them. There was no doubt that

---

11 **cavort**: jump happily around   19 **clear off**: go away   25 **evenly**: with
a controlled voice   56 **let sb. off**: not punish sb.   64 **blurt sth. out**: etwas
heraussprudeln   65 **sort sb. out**: (here) beat sb. up   66 **dissuade sb.**: convince sb.
not to do sth.

the spirit of the party was now dampened and that nothing would revive it. Then Zoot spoke, more to himself although the rest were listening.

'You know, it's a funny thing, but it's only in the District that I feel safe. District Six is like an island, if you follow me, an island in a sea of apartheid. The whole of District Six is one big apartheid, so we can't see it. We only see it when the white man comes and forces it on us, when he makes us see it – when the police come, and the council people and so on – or when we leave the District, when we leave our island and go into Cape Town or to Sea Point or come here to Kalk Bay. Then we again see apartheid. I know the District is dirty and poor and a slum, as the newspapers always remind us, but it's our own and we have never put up notices which say "Slegs blankes" or "Whites only". *They* put up the notices. When the white man comes into the District with his notices he is a stranger, and when we come out of the District he makes us realise that we are strangers. It's funny but that's the way I see it.'

This was more than he had spoken for a long time, and the rest of the party did not interrupt or comment.

'Well, that's that. Now I suggest we have a last drink, pack up our things, and get the hell back to the District as soon as we can.'

They took an empty train back while crowded trains were still coming in.

Pastor Bruintjies

Whenever Mary called a meeting at the Casbah it was an emergency meeting. It was seldom that she found it necessary to do so but, when it was, it meant that something serious was happening or about to happen. One Sunday afternoon, just two weeks before Christmas, she called such a meeting. She sat gloomily at the head of her dining-room table with the Casbah girls on her left and the Winsor Park boys on her right.

Not much had changed at Buckingham Palace during the five years before. The Abrahams and Knight families still lived there although threats of forced removal had now become more ominous. Mary was still the Madam in charge of the Casbah, with The Butterfly and Moena Mooies, a bit older, more experienced and weather-beaten, still working for her. Fiela Vreters had left. One of her customers, a butcher's delivery-man who used to drop in between meat rounds, had made her pregnant but was decent enough to want the baby and so married her. They moved into a council house in Kewtown, where a son was born, large and meaty like his father. In Fiela's place came Miss Sophie. No-one knew what her surname was or even whether she had one, but she had been a secretary to a dentist and could type. She gave the impression of being prim and correct when off duty but was a vixen when on duty and she had taken off her spectacles. She insisted on always being addressed, whether on duty or off, as Miss Sophie.

The Boys at Winsor Park had also lost one and gained another. Zoot was still the leader, and his sparkle was as effervescent as ever. He was the one who paid Katzen the rent, which he had not done since he had first moved in years before. Oubaas and Pretty-Boy were still with him, the latter as youthful and blue-eyed as ever. Boere had left as suddenly as he had come. After their first party, five years before, when he had been found dead-drunk on the lavatory seat, he had become a permanent

---

1 **dampened** (adj): gedämpft   **revive sth.**: bring sth. back to life   19 **get the hell back** (infml): go back as quickly as possible   30 **forced removal**: Zwangs-umsiedlung   **ominous**: drohend   40 **prim**: over-correct   **vixen**: female fox; (here) sexually exciting   44 **effervescent**: sprudelnd

member of Winsor Park. After the last party, a few months before, he had also ended up drunk on the lavatory seat, but this time when he woke up he pulled the chain, left the toilet and the house, and was never seen in Winsor Park again.

In his place Surprise Arendse moved in. He was a huge man, well over six foot and very muscular, with the temperament of a cherub. His mother, from whom he inherited his height and build, had worked as a farm-hand in the Boland. She had been unaware that she was pregnant until a month before her son arrived. She was so surprised that that was what she called him. He left the farm while still a towering youth and drifted into Cape Town where he met Pretty-Boy on the Grand Parade. He came back with him to Winsor Park and stayed. Now he worked as a part-time bouncer at the Casbah. He hardly bounced anyone but could be dangerous when finally aroused.

Mary called the meeting to order and produced a letter from her father. Pastor Adam Bruintjies wrote that he would be celebrating his seventieth birthday on Tuesday, 27 December, and would like to spend it quietly with his only daughter at her boarding-house in Cape Town. His sister, with whom he usually stayed in Walmer Estate, had gone on a vacation to Durban, so he had nowhere else to go. He would be driving in that morning, have his annual medical check-up at Groote Schuur hospital in the afternoon, do some shopping and visit friends afterwards, and arrive in Caledon Street at 7 p.m. Since Mary's place was a boarding-house, he was booking a room with bath or shower well in advance. He would vacate it before noon the following day. All he required was one night's bed and breakfast and the singular pleasure of being with his daughter.

Pastor Bruintjies was now retired and quietly growing roses in his garden at home. He still lived at the mission station parsonage. Mary visited him annually at *Kinderfees*. She then wore sober black, attended church service, visited her mother's grave and was the epitome of respectability. Whether this impressed her father was not easy to say, although it certainly pleased him. He never referred to her business in Cape Town and gave the impression that he found no reason to disbelieve her story that she ran a boarding-house.

He in his turn only came to Cape Town once a year on his birthday. He usually stayed overnight with his religious spinster sister in her small, semi-detached house in Queen's Road. This was the same sister

with whom Mary had first boarded when she came to the city. Now they only met once a year on the evening of 27 December, when Mary went
40 to have dinner there to celebrate her father's birthday. She would mumble a greeting to her aunt, kiss her father whom she genuinely loved, hand him a present and speak only to him for the rest of the evening. Whenever Pastor Adam suggested that he stay with her at her boarding-house, Mary would invent some excuse. Either the place was fully booked or
45 some major renovation was taking place. Her aunt always pulled up her nose at the mention of 'boarding-house' and snorted something which sounded like 'bawdy house'. The pun seemed lost on Pastor Bruintjies or perhaps he chose to ignore it. One couldn't tell with him.

An air of gloom hung over Mary's meeting after they had heard the
50 letter. There was long pause.

'So then, what can be done about it?' Zoot asked helplessly.

Mary did not answer but stared blankly at him.

'Maybe you can write and tell him that the place is being painted.'

'I told him that last year.'
55 'Or the roof is being repaired.'

'I told him that the year before.'

'Maybe you can go to Durban on a holiday,' Pretty-Boy suggested desperately.

'And run into that witch of an aunt of mine with her bible tracts?'
60 The silence crept back over the assembly.

Oubaas struggled to speak. He grinned foolishly at himself and said, 'If it's birthday, then why don't we accept it as such, invite him, and give him a party here? It's only a suggestion,' he concluded lamely.

There was a look of amazement on all faces. Pretty-Boy was the first
65 to recover.

'Oubaas,' he said with genuine feeling, 'I have always known that there are times when you are a genius.'

---

6 **cherub**: angel   10 **towering**: very tall   15 **produce sth.**: take sth. out   24 **well in advance**: a long time before   25 **vacate sth.**: move out of sth.   26 **singular**: special   28 **parsonage**: priest's home   30 **epitome** [ɪˈpɪtəmi]: perfect example   36 **spinster**: unmarried   37 **semi-detached house**: Doppelhaushälfte   45–46 **pull up your nose**: die Nase rümpfen   46 **snort**: schnauben   47 **bawdy house**: brothel

Ideas now spilled over. Pastor Bruintjies was going to get the surprise party of his life. A guest list was immediately compiled and intensely argued about. Miss Sophie was instructed to type and send off the invitations. The Butterfly would see to the music and The Boys fix up a bar on the back porch. 5

'We must have romantic music for atmosphere,' Miss Sophie suggested.

'And cocktails in long glasses,' The Butterfly stated.

'And bits of viennas and cheese punctured with toothpicks,' Pretty-Boy concluded.

Neighbours and others on the guest list were sent typed invitations. The 10 Reverend Father Rowland and the principal of the school, Mr Theo Plaatjies B.A., were invited to lend class to the proceedings. Katzen was also asked as were Mr and Mrs Angelo Baptiste. And so was Moodley; there was a long argument about which of his three wives should be invited.

The Girls bought dress material from Katzen and spent all their spare 15 time designing, cutting and sewing new party frocks. The Boys admitted reluctantly that they had no clothes worthy of the occasion. Zoot's old check suit no longer fitted and his Jarmans had long ago been discarded. Pretty-Boy had the answer to the problems. He still had a friend who could find all the clothes they needed at a bargain price. Pretty-Boy had 20 a legion of friends who could supply anything to him at a bargain price. What that price was no-one asked since no-one ever considered paying. No-one had ever seen these friends but Pretty-Boy. This friend this time, as always, was true to his word and Pretty-Boy started bringing home clothes. At first there was the merest trickle but this grew into a veritable 25 flood. He brought home an assortment of suits including a tuxedo, and tails that fitted Surprise perfectly. One evening he brought home a complete Teddy-boy outfit for himself. Some of the jackets and trousers still had on price tags, others still retained their dry-cleaning labels. Many of the shirts were still wrapped in cellophane while others were 30 still on hangers. There were boxes and boxes of shoes. Finally The Boys were all decked out to their satisfaction.

Early on the afternoon of 27 December, the Casbah was closed for business. All preparations were complete. The red light over the front door was removed and coloured lights strung over the bar. Those guests 35 who had arrived early were sworn to secrecy and let into the conspiracy.

At 7 p.m. a young man was the only person to be seen lounging on the stoep of 201. He wore the latest Teddy-boy outfit of a velvet-collared, purple, draped jacket, drain-pipe trousers and a thin string tie. His blue
40 suede shoes matched the innocent blue of his eyes. He watched carefully as an old Dodge with a country registration coughed and spluttered slowly from Tennant Street. The young man gave a low whistle and all the lights at the Casbah were switched off immediately and the house plunged into darkness. The car rattled up and with a jolt pulled to a
45 stop. Pastor Bruintjies turned down the window and spoke to the man on the stoep.

'I'm looking for 201. It's a boarding-house.'

'This is 201.'

'Doesn't look like a boarding-house to me. Seems all in darkness.
50 Who lives here?'

'Miss Mary.'

'Then it must be the place. That's the name. I'm her father.'

'Miss Mary must be home. That's her Austin there, the blue car. I think they're most probably all at the back. Why don't you just walk
55 through and see?'

'You think it will be all right?'

'Sure it will be all right.'

Pastor Bruintjies creakingly eased himself out of his car. He tried the front door and to his surprise found it unlocked. He opened it. He was
60 blinded by all the house lights being switched on at the same time.

---

2 **compile sth.**: put sth. (esp. a list) together   4 **see to sth.**: take care of sth.
8 **vienna**: Schnitzel   9 **conclude**: bring the discussion to an end   12 **lend class to sth.**: give sth. more prestige   17 **worthy of the occasion**: dem Anlass angemessen   18 **discarded**: ausgemustert   25 **trickle**: small quantity that arrives slowly   **veritable**: true   26 **tuxedo** [tʌk'siːdəʊ]: dinner jacket   27 **tails** (pl): Frack
28 **Teddy-boy**: youth style in dress in the 1950s   32 **be decked out**: be dressed neatly   36 **swear sb. to secrecy**: jdn. zur Geheimhaltung verpflichten   37 **lounge**: lie around   38 **velvet-collared**: mit einem Samtkragen   39 **draped jacket**: loses Jackett   **drain-pipe trousers**: narrow trousers   40 **suede** [sweɪd]: Wildleder
41 **country registration**: number plate from outside Cape Town   **splutter**: stottern
44 **rattle**: shake   **with a jolt**: mit einem Ruck   58 **creak**: quietschen   **ease yourself out of sth.**: get out of sth. slowly

When he recovered he saw his daughter Mary, resplendent in a pink gown, standing with a bottle of opened champagne. She was surrounded by people all holding glasses. A huge man in a tailcoat held a tray filled with glasses and champagne. Against a wall a banner was strung which read 'God Bless You, Pastor Adam'. Then everybody together sang 5 'Happy Birthday to You'.

Pastor Bruintjies recovered after he had downed two glasses of champagne in rapid succession. There was toast after toast drunk to him. Mary said something and a man he later discovered was Mr Theo Plaatjies B.A. made a long, involved speech in English. Then a pretty 10 sixteen-year-old girl called Faith Knight curtsied and presented him with a birthday present on behalf of the people of Buckingham Palace. He unwrapped the box and drew out a dark-red silk dressing-gown. On it the letters PB had been embroidered in gold by The Butterfly. Pastor Bruintjies was prevailed upon to put on the gown right there, which he 15 did. Then Mary took him around introducing him to the assembly. There were so many names and so many different faces. Oubaas, The Butterfly (who gave him a resounding kiss to the cheers of all), Moena Mooies, a Miss Sophie, Mr Zoot and Pretty-Boy (the man in the Teddy-boy outfit on the stoep). And the neighbours. Mr and Mrs Abrahams 20 and their daughter Moena, who lived two houses up. Mr and Mrs Knight, the parents of the pretty girl who had given him the present. There was also a surly little white man who was introduced as Mr Katzen, the landlord. He was talking to a quiet, round Italian and his voluble, round wife, who were introduced as Mr and Mrs Angelo 25 Baptiste. Standing with them was a tall, silent Indian shopkeeper, Mr Moodley, and a pale apparition with a dot on her forehead, his wife.

Mr Theo Plaatjies B.A. nervously took the pastor aside and engaged him in a learned conversation about the teaching of comprehension at the junior secondary school level. When Father Rowland arrived, 30 apologising for being late, he joined in the discussion, which then took a decidedly theological direction.

Surprise, resplendent in his tails, was an excellent wine and spirits waiter. Pastor Bruintjies was his special concern. He served him whisky after whisky in style. By now the pastor had dispensed with being 35 intellectual and was roaring with laughter with The Butterfly and Pretty-Boy. The Jungle Boys arrived with a pile of records, were introduced to

the guest of honour and retired to a corner where they took control of
the radiogram and music.

40   The party was being pleasant, respectable and dull. By eleven o'clock
most of the older people had left. Father Rowland had a sermon to
prepare and Mr Theo Plaatjies B.A. was completing an article on remedial
education for the Principals' Association. The Abrahamses and the
Knights had also left. Mr and Mrs Moodley, Mr and Mrs Baptiste and Mr
45 Katzen had left much earlier.

    The party began recovering slightly. Zoot tried to persuade Pastor
Bruintjies to do tap-dancing. Mary got out her neglected baton, wiped
off the dust, and started twirling it as if she had never forgotten the art.
Surprise kept plying her father with whisky which was never refused.

50   Just before midnight four Portuguese sailors off a boat in the Duncan
Dock gate-crashed, looking for girls and waving bottles of wine and
money. The Jungle Boys, smelling blood, geared into action. There
followed a tremendous battle in which, assisted by Surprise in his tails,
they launched charge after charge. Pastor Bruintjies, magnificent in his
55 red gown, urged on the Casbah forces with Mary's baton. Finally the
sailors were expelled at the expense of a blue eye for Toyer, a broken
table-leg and two smashed chairs.

    Star Bioscope came out and three dagga-dizzy members of the
Naughty Boys gang tried to force their way into the party. While they
60 were being driven out, the Portuguese sailors came back with
reinforcements and teamed up with the Naughty Boys. There was
another great battle and this time two windows were broken and the
front door left hanging on one hinge. While Pastor Bruintjies was
marshalling and urging on his forces he was felled by a tray of savouries
65 hurled at him by a Naughty Boy. He was up again almost immediately
and dizzily encouraging the combined forces of The Jungles and Winsor

11 **curtsy**: einen Knicks machen   14 **embroidered**: gestickt   18 **resounding**: very
loud   25 **voluble**: talkative   27 **pale apparition**: like a ghost   38 **retire**: (here)
go and stay somewhere alone   42-43 **remedial education**: education for slow
learners   49 **ply sb. with sth.**: provide sb. with sth.   51 **gate-crash**: enter without
an invitation   58 **bioscope came out**: the cinema closed   **dagga-dizzy**: under the
influence of cannabis   63 **hinge**: Scharnier   64 **marshal sth.**: organize sth.
fell sb.: knock sb. down

Park with mayonnaise and sardines dripping from his cut forehead. Two police vans screeched to a halt and after lengthy explanations loaded up the Portuguese and drove them back to the docks.

Morning found Mary blubbering to herself on the floor among the wreckage. Her gown was soiled and the banner torn from the wall. The dining-room table was balancing on three legs, chairs were smashed and broken glass scattered everywhere. In addition her father was missing. The Girls were sleeping in one another's arms on the dining-room floor and the Boys were snoring on the back porch. Mary was the only one awake. Tearfully she got up to fetch a broom, gave up the effort and sank back onto the floor.

Then the front door swung open on its only hinge and Pastor Bruintjies came in followed by Zoot. Each had a bottle of whisky and a glass. The pastor was still wearing his dressing-gown, now stained and torn, and had a piece of white crêpe paper flapping around his head as a makeshift bandage. He was laughing and in high spirits. He had spent the entire night drinking and discussing with Zoot.

'This man is a born philosopher, a genius if ever there was one. He has told me things about guardian angels I had never thought possible. Nothing in my theological training has prepared me for this. Mr Milton Zoot,' he said, unsteadily extending his hand, 'I greet you!'

Mary looked up in tearful amazement.

'And I must also thank my wonderful and only daughter for the magnificent party she gave for her poor old father. This is the best birthday I have ever had,' he said. 'My daughter, I kiss you.'

He bent down to do so, sank down onto the floor next to Mary and passed out.

It was well after midday that he awoke. He was most reluctant to leave for the Boland and tried to persuade Zoot to come with him and be his guest for ever. He threatened that, if not, he would move into Winsor Park. He promised to return to celebrate all his birthdays at Mary's boarding-house till he was a hundred years old. He loved the girls, especially The Butterfly. He loved the boys and admired Zoot, but most of all he loved his daughter Mary. Zoot, he was prepared to tell everyone, was the greatest intellectual he had ever met.

Finally he was tidied up and dressed. Clutching the box containing his torn dressing-gown, he was persuaded to get into his car. The engine rattled alive. As he pulled away he winked an eye conspiratorially at his daughter while chuckling happily to himself.

2 **screech to a halt**: stop noisily   4 **blubber** (infml): weep; cry   5 **wreckage**: broken furniture etc.   **soiled**: dirty   27 **pass out**: ohnmächtig werden
38 **conspiratorial**: verschwörerisch   39 **chuckle**: laugh quietly

Mr O'Grady

The church held two major functions every year. There were numerous smaller ones such as the pancake evening and the big walk, but the big ones, the ones that everyone spoke about for weeks before the time, came at the end of October and on Easter Saturday. The bazaar was held in October and the Grand Ball at Easter. The bazaar, although a major 5 event, was modest by comparison with the Easter affair. The bazaar was held in the school hall whereas the ball was a lavish occasion in the Woodstock Town Hall with everyone in formal dress and Stand Murray and his Exotic Band in attendance.

Many in the District patronised the bazaar but everyone worth 10 anything attended the ball. The highlight of the evening was the crowning of Miss District Six and her two princesses by Councillor Mrs Desai. Besides instant fame, the winner had her photograph, with her princesses on either side, on the social page of the *Argus* and she received a free boat-trip for two on a Union-Castle liner to Durban and back 15 sponsored by Gowell Travel Agency. The first princess was given a tea-service generously donated by Katzen, and the second princess free hair shampoos for six months by Mr Henry Knight, who was also chief convener of the beauty competition.

What always proved to be his worst headache was to find a panel of 20 three willing enough to judge. The preliminaries were usually held a week before at a function in the school hall. The contestants paraded in casual wear, swim wear and evening dresses. The winners were announced a week later at the Grand Ball in the Woodstock Town Hall with Mr Stan Murray playing sympathetic background music. 25

The contest was taken so seriously that no judge could afford to give an unpopular decision. One such judge, now seldom spoken of, had had the temerity to select a girl from Bo-Kaap who did not even belong to the church. He was never allowed to set foot in the District again. This year Mr Theo Plaatjies B.A., under tremendous pressure, had 30 reluctantly consented to convene the panel. No-one on his staff, not even the caretaker, no official of the church, not even the collector of church dues, was prepared to serve on it with him. After approaching several persons, all of whom made some excuse, he finally found Zoot

35 willing and even his acceptance was conditional: 'If you want me, you ask my friend Pretty-Boy as well.' The latter was in ecstasy when approached and consented immediately, excited at what effect his look would have on so many beautiful women.

Early on the evening of the preliminary competition, the three judges
40 convened for the first time in the principal's office. Mr Theo Plaatjies B.A. felt it necessary to clarify his position immediately.

'Gentlemen, this is not the sort of thing I prefer doing. I've never been involved in something like this before. I'm not even sure why I consented to convene this panel. But if it is for the good of our church
45 and school, then who am I to refuse? Now, how do we set about it? Come, gentlemen, I am relying on your greater experience.'

'I think it is obvious,' Zoot said. 'We select those with the pretties faces.'

'What about the figure? And then what about lower down?' Pretty-
50 Boy asked scornfully, for once challenging his boss. Pretty-Boy knew when he was on safe ground. 'You may start with the face but sooner or later you must get to the sweet-melons, if you know what I'm getting at, Mr Plaatjies. The bigger their sweet-melons the better their chances.'

He indicated the size he thought suitable by stretching his fingers to
55 their limit.

'After that we can go lower down.'

'Yes, yes,' the principal agreed, 'but it might be easier if we gave a popular decision.'

'What's that?' Pretty-Boy asked suspiciously.

60 'We judge the winner by the volume of applause she gets. The one who gets the loudest cheers wins, the next loudest becomes the first princess, and so on.'

'And what about the size of the sweet-melons?' Pretty-Boy asked contemptuously.

---

7 **lavish**: luxurious 10 **patronise sth.**: go to sth. because you feel you ought to
19 **convener**: organizer 21 **preliminaries**: first rounds 23 **casual wear**: informal
clothes 28 **temerity**: nerve 37 **approach sb.**: go and ask sb. 45 **How do we set
about it?**: How do we do it? 50 **scornful**: höhnisch

The principal chose to ignore him. 'If we give such a decision, we might survive. We will certainly not be unpopular with everyone.'

'How can you judge by clapping,' Pretty-Boy jumped back into the fray. 'It's not fair. You can ignore the face, but not the sweet-melons.'

'Gentlemen, we will give a popular decision,' the principal repeated tight-lipped.

They entered the crowded hall.

Mr Knight, resplendent in tuxedo, introduced the judges to the audience.

'Firstly, ladies and gentlemen, the chairman of the judges panel, the principal of our school, Mr Theo Plaatjies B.A.' The principal rose nervously to polite applause.

'Next we have a man of wide experience, whom we have all known for a very long time, Mr September.' Zoot was dressed in the suit he had worn to Pastor Bruintjie's party. There was loud applause.

'And last but not least, to bring youth and energy to wisdom and experience, we have Mr Vermeulen.' Pretty-Boy was wearing his Teddy-boy outfit. There was deafening applause.

As the judges seated themselves in the front row, Pretty-Boy whispered to Zoot, 'Have you noticed that there seem to be no men in the audience, only women and children.'

Zoot looked around cautiously. 'You're damn right. Not even Oubaas or Surprise. Where the hell can they all be?'

The ladies paraded in casual wear.

'There should have been an age limit,' Zoot whispered.

'They should have refused anybody over forty,' Pretty-Boy added.

Then they paraded in bathing-costumes.

'There should have been a weight limit,' Zoot whispered.

'When I spoke of sweet-melons, this is not what I meant,' Pretty-Boy added.

Finally they paraded in evening wear.

'I can't see a single winner,' Zoot whispered desperately.

'Neither can I,' Pretty-Boy added.

'We will take a popular decision,' Mr Theo Plaatjies B.A. said with finality.

Mr Knight made an announcement that the final decision would be announced at the Grand Ball in the Woodstock Town Hall. As he was

leaving the hall with the judges, a small, bird-like white man with a
gammy leg joined them. He was introduced as Mr Patrick O'Grady,
40   sidesman and member of the church council.

    'Yes, can't you see? I'm Irish to the core,' he said. 'I used to live in the
District but now live in Silvertown. But I still come all the way to worship
at my old church. Regular Orangeman I used to be from Country Kerry.'
Zoot and Pretty-Boy stared at him, but he continued twittering away
45   unabashed. 'We all owe a debt of thanks to you people for sacrificing
your evening like this. I thought the girls were gorgeous. What did you
think?'

    They thought him mad.

    'I need a drink badly,' Zoot remarked to no-one in particular.

50   'Me too,' Pretty-Boy agreed.

    'You really need a drink?' Mr O'Grady asked.

    'My need is desperate,' Zoot said.

    'Why didn't you say so earlier. Come on then. The men are all
enjoying themselves in the vestry.'

55   The room was crowded and drink was flowing freely. Surprise was
conducting a group of raucous singers, a cassock draped askew over his
shoulders. Oubaas was giggling inanely and greeted Zoot like a long-last
brother. Father Rowland genially collared the principal.

    'How did it go? I don't suppose we can know yet who the winners
60   are?'

    'We will take a popular decision,' Mr Plaatjies B.A. replied as a glass
of whisky was thrust into his hand.

    Mr O'Grady was everywhere, cheeping away to everyone who would
listen to him. Finally he joined a group in which Zoot and the principal
65   were standing.

---

6 **tight-lipped**: verkniffen   18 **deafening**: very loud   39 **gammy**: damaged, injured
40 **sidesman**: church official   41 **to the core**: through and through   43 **Orangeman**: Irish Protestant in favour of the union with Great Britain   45 **unabashed**:
unerschrocken   **debt of thanks**: Dankesschuld   56 **conduct sth.**: lead sth. (esp.
an orchestra)   **raucous** ['rɔːkəs]: unpleasantly noisy   **a cassock draped askew**:
eine schief drapierte Soutane   57 **giggle inanely**: make a stupid laughing sound
58 **collar sb.**: jdn. schnappen   **genially**: freundlich   63 **cheep away**: chat

'Don't mean to intrude,' he said addressing Mr Plaatjies, 'but I'm looking for a lift home. Don't suppose you are going my way, are you?'

'I don't think I know what your way is? I live in Walmer Estate.'

'I'm not far out of your way. Silvertown. I'm afraid I've missed the last bus.'   5

'Oh dear, I suppose if you are stranded I could give you a lift.'

'It's most kind of you. You must say if I'm inconveniencing you.'

'Not at all. It will be my pleasure.'

Mr O'Grady twittered over to another group.

'For goodness sake please go with me,' the principal implored Zoot,   10
'that man will talk me to death.'

'O.K. by me, if my pal Mr Pretty-Boy Vermeulen can go along.'

'Anyone you like. I'll bring you home afterwards. Only don't leave me with that terrible man.'

All the way to Silvertown Mr O'Grady chirped away. He told them he   15
had left college in Dublin before completing a teacher's course, and quoted from *The Education Handbook* and the *Rubaiyat* to prove his point. He had come to South Africa working on board a ship and disembarked at Durban, where he met an Indian girl whom he later married. Those were the days before this damn Immorality Act, he said.   20
He and his wife were still happily married and still living together in spite of the law. They and their children lived in a council house right in the middle of Silvertown. (Turn left at the robot, Professor Plaatjies.) He had no prejudices and nothing but contempt for those white people who had. Such people had no right to call themselves Europeans. No   25
decent European could still have prejudice and be a European. (We turn right at the second robot, Professor Plaatjies.) His wife was Indian and had beautiful long hair. (Up this street, Professor Plaatjies.) They had eight children, six boys and two girls. Elvis the eldest was eighteen and Patrick the youngest was now five. (Slower now, it's up the next street,   30
Professor Plaatjies.)

They drew up outside a small council house which was all in darkness. Mr O'Grady insisted that they come in to meet his wife and have a drink. He was not going to get out of the car unless they consented. Mr Plaatjies complained about the lateness of the hour. Zoot   35
and Pretty-Boy were quite willing to have the offered drink.

The tiny lounge was strewn with sleeping bodies lying on mattresses on the floor. Mr O'Grady limping ahead picked his way gingerly over his many children. The rest followed him less successfully. He took them
40 into a small room where his wife was sitting up in bed combing her hair. The youngest O'Grady, Patrick, was fast asleep next to her in the corner. The principal and Zoot sat down on two chairs offered to them, and Pretty-Boy cleared a space for himself on the dressing-table. Mr O'Grady introduced his guests with a flourish.

45 'My learned friend Professor Plaatjies B.A., Mr September and Mr Vermeulen. My wife Mrs Thingalangam O'Grady. I would like to offer you gentlemen a drink but I don't think I have a drop left in the house. However, there's an excellent shebeen round the corner if the professor could favour me with a small loan.'

50 The principal took out his wallet.

'Five pounds will do nicely,' Mr O'Grady said. 'You must remind me to pay you back. Elvis!' he shouted and his eldest son, who was still awake, came in from the next room. He had long sideburns.

'Go round the corner to Miley's and see if you can get a bottle of Old
55 Brown,' he ordered.

His father explained that everyone called his son Elvis. He had an electric guitar and could play, dance and sing just like Elvis Presley. He had already won two talent contests.

Elvis returned and there was a quick, sharp altercation between
60 father and son about the change, which O'Grady finally pocketed. Drinks were poured all round but Mr Plaatjies declined as he was driving and the hour late – or early, as he said sarcastically.

Then Elvis was prevailed upon to do his turn. He fetched his guitar, plugged it in and gave a noisy and enthusiastic rendition of 'I'm All
65 Shook Up'.

---

7 **inconvenience sb.**: make life difficult for sb.   12 **pal** (infml): friend
19 **disembark**: get off a ship   20 **Immorality Act**: law (1949) forbidding marriage
or sexual contact between different racial groups   23 **robot** (SAE): traffic lights
24 **contempt**: Verachtung   37 **strewn**: verstreut   38 **limp**: hinken   53 **sideburns**
(pl): Koteletten   59 **altercation**: disagreement   61 **decline**: say no   63 **turn**:
(hier) Nummer

The principal said he was going to get sick and the noise was not doing him any good. He must go outside immediately for some fresh air. Could Zoot help him? He was looking pale and stood up unsteadily. As Zoot assisted him outside, they found all the O'Gradys up and dancing to Elvis's music as if their lives depended on it. Zoot left Mr Plaatjies B.A. 5 to get sick on his own, and returned to join Pretty-Boy at the impromptu party.

The youngest O'Grady, Patrick, who had been woken by the noise, stumbled in half asleep and was persuaded to do his turn. With Elvis strumming in the background he sang 'Moon River' like Danny Williams. 10 Then Zoot gave a tap-dancing display, during which Pretty-Boy mesmerised the O'Grady girls with his good looks and innocent blue eyes.

At three o'clock, after repeated complaints from the neighbours, the party came to a reluctant end and everyone went outside in search of the 15 principal. They found Mr Theo Plaatjies B.A. fast asleep in his car.

'Professor,' Pretty-Boy chirped in imitation of O'Grady, 'I think it is time that we left.'

'We'll take a popular decision,' the principal mumbled.

When finally woken, he adjusted his clothes and started his car. They 20 pulled away to cheers from all the O'Gradys, who were clustered in the middle of the road.

Elvis

Easter Saturday evening anyone who was anyone dressed to the gills
and converged on the Woodstock Town Hall from District Six and even
25 beyond. Surprise was the doorman and already early in position. He
was impressive in tails and bow-tie, although the total effect was marred
by his footwear, a pair of soiled white tackies. As guests arrived they
handed their tickets to him and with a flourish he tore these in half. The
hall was festooned with crêpe paper and multi-coloured balloons. Stan
30 Murray and his Exotic Band were playing mood music softly in order to
set the right atmosphere.

    Mr Joseph Knight, a very fussy and precise compère, had also arrived
early with his wife and pretty daughter, and he was now darting around
checking fastidiously on the finishing touches. This was Faith's first
35 grown-up ball and she wore a dress that was a froth of pink and white
taffeta. Zoot and all the Boys were on duty. Besides Surprise at the door,
Zoot and Pretty-Boy were masters of ceremonies whose work it was to
introduce shy couples to each other. Oubaas was in his element as
assistant barman. Mr and Mrs Abrahams, their daughter Moena and the
40 Jungle Boys arrived slightly later in the Globe Furnishers delivery van
driven by Amaai, who was now chief storeman at the firm. Then a blue
Austin drew up and Surprise handsomely rushed to open the car door.
The Girls got out stylishly. They were dressed as flappers of the 1920s,
complete with headbands, short dresses with dropped waistlines, black
45 fishnet stockings and cigarettes in long holders. Then Mary grandly

---

9 **stumble**: stolpern   10 **strum**: klimpern   12 **mesmerise sb.**: have a strong effect
on sb. so that they cannot concentrate on anything else   21 **clustered**: standing in
a group   23 **dress to the gills**: put on your fanciest clothes   24 **converge on sth.**:
go to sth.   26 **bow-tie**: Fliege   **mar sth.**: spoil sth.   27 **tackies** (infml): sports
shoes   29 **festoon sth.**: decorate sth.   32 **fussy**: over-correct   33 **dart around**:
run around   34 **fastidious**: extremely careful   **the finishing touches**: der letzte
Schliff   35 **froth**: Schaum   37 **master of ceremonies**: Conferencier   42 **draw up**:
stop **handsomely**: (here) in a graceful way   43 **flapper**: fashionable girl of the
1920s   44 **waistline**: Taille

emerged. She wore a full black frock, as befitted her status, with an ostrich-feather boa draped loosely around her neck.

Car after car pulled up. Mr Theo Plaatjies B.A. came with his pale, anaemic-looking wife. Then the Reverend Father Rowland drew up with the guest of honour, Councillor Mrs Desai, daughter of a famous father, 5 who was renowned throughout Cape Town as a fiery fighter for justice. By the time the Exotics had struck up the first dance, the bar was doing a roaring trade. Zoot gallantly gave his arm to Mary and led her onto the dance floor. Pretty-Boy then prevailed on the shy Moena Lelik to accompany him in a slow foxtrot. The next dance was a waltz, and Zoot 10 ostentatiously requested the pleasure of that one with Miss Faith Knight. She was an excited and happy whirl of pink and white as she glided with him across the floor.

Pretty-Boy was smoking in the yard while chatting to Oubaas when a young man, already slightly drunk, eyed him and then introduced himself. 15

'Remember me?'

Pretty-Boy looked hard but did not recognise him, although the sideburns looked familiar.

'It's me, Johnny O'Grady.'

Pretty-Boy was still puzzled. The youth mimed playing a guitar, sang 20 the opening bar of 'I'm All Shook Up', and did a rock-'n-roll step.

'Elvis?' Pretty-Boy asked hesitantly.

'Sure thing. The one and only. Silvertown's answer to Elvis Presley. How you doing, Mr Pretty-Boy? Long time no see.'

'Yes, of course, I remember the night we spent at your place.' 25

'I brought dad tonight in my jalopy. It' s a Volksie,' he said proudly. 'I've got a job now. Plenty cash. Could I offer you a drink, Mr Pretty-Boy?'

From his pocket he produced a hip-flask from which Pretty-Boy took a swig of whisky. 30

'I wonder if you could do me a special favour and introduce me to that lovely chick Mr Zoot was dancing with.' He indicated Faith, who was talking animatedly to her mother. 'After all that's your job here, isn't it?'

Pretty-Boy did not like his tone and started feeling uncomfortable in his presence. Nevertheless he took him over and introduced Mr Johnny 35 O'Grady to mother and daughter.

'Could I have the next dance?'

Faith was flattered. There were far too many older people at the ball.
Her mother reluctantly consented but made it clear that she was not
40 very happy about Elvis.

'Only this one, Faith, you know you mustn't overdo things. Me and
your father are always saying so.'

They danced that one and the next after Mrs Knight was called away
to help supervise the catering. After that the couple ignored everyone
45 else at the ball. Faith had eyes only for her partner. After an exhausting
samba he bought two cokes and suggested that they drink them outside
in his car.

'It's bitter,' Faith said in the car, pulling a face at the coke.

'It's got a little something in to make a little girl I know love me
50 tender.'

She grimaced and swallowed. They went back and danced together
until Mr Knight announced the intermission. His wife had obviously
spoken to him because he gave his daughter an annoyed glance. Elvis
suggested that Faith and he go outside to avoid the boring speeches.

55 Father Rowland came on the stage to a roll of drums from the Exotics.
He thanked everyone for supporting the ball, then introduced Councillor
Mrs Desai, 'a legend in her lifetime like her father' as he referred to her.
The Councillor's address was a torrent of political fire. She concluded by
telling the guests that the move to have District Six declared a white
60 group area was a shameful one. They would soon receive letters to
appear before the Board. They must ignore these. They must remain in
their homes until the bulldozers surrounded them. They had built
District Six. They were District Six. And the white man must realise that
in no uncertain manner.

65 There was deafening applause when she concluded and the
Councillor was presented with a bouquet of flowers. It was to have been

---

1 **frock**: dress   **as befits sb.'s status**: as is correct for sb.'s social position
2 **ostrich-feather boa**: Straußenfederboa   12 **glide**: schweben   26 **jalopy** (old-
fashioned sl): car   30 **swig**: Schluck   58 **torrent**: Schwall   64 **in no uncertain
manner**: loud and clear

handed over to her by Faith, but to her parent's annoyance, the girl was nowhere to be found.

Mr Knight took over from Father Rowland. Mr O'Grady, unsteady with drink, swayed slightly next to him. Mr Knight introduced the convener of the beauty competition panel, Mr Theo Plaatjies B.A. who in turn introduced his fellow judges and then said tersely, 'After a lengthy discussion we have decided to give a popular decision.' It was given amid popular applause. The middle-aged queen heavily mounted her throne flanked by her two middle-aged princesses. They were crowned by a beaming Councillor Mrs Desai.

'I can't take any more of this,' Pretty-Boy said to himself. 'Can anyone imagine any beauty queen with sweet-melons that size? I'm going outside to get sick.'

As he stood at the door complaining to Surprise, who grinned in sympathy, a red Volkswagen pulled away with a laughing couple inside.

'That's young Miss Faith and her boy-friend,' Surprise said.

'Elvis?' Pretty-Boy asked.

'I don't know his name, but he's got long sideburns and sat drinking with her all the time in that car. I wanted to warn her but then again it isn't my business.'

The guests now enjoyed what the invitations referred to as a finger supper. This consisted of fried chicken and assorted salads served on paper plates. After desserts of jelly and custard, the intermission was over and the Exotics struck up a lively quadrille. Mr Plaatjies was the enthusiastic leader of his square and showed an amazing turn of energy as he shouted commands, 'Arm in arm! Now swing your partners! Back again! Change! *Nou huistoe*!' He had lost any inhibitions he might have had. His pale wife, who was his partner, showed even more energy.

Later that evening a worried Mrs Knight asked Zoot whether he had seen Faith. He remembered seeing her earlier but not after the supper. She then asked Mary. She had last spoken to her some time before the speeches. Then Mrs Knight asked Pretty-Boy. Without replying he took her over to Surprise at the door.

'Tell Mrs Knight where Faith went.'

'I don't really know, madam. Me and Pretty-Boy here saw her drive off with that chap with the long sideburns in his red Volksie. They can't be back yet or I would have seen that car. I didn't like the guy. Didn't look the right sort to me.'

They searched for Mr O'Grady senior and found him dead-drunk
40 groaning on a bench in the yard.

At 2 a.m. the Exotics played 'Auld Lang Syne' and the Grand Ball was officially over for that year. Faith was not back yet. By now Mrs Knight was frantic and she and her husband drove to the local police station to report their daughter missing. The Boys decided on joint action with
45 The Jungles and piled into the Globe Furnishers van in which they drove off speedily in search of the red Volkswagen.

Mary and The Girls arrived back at the Casbah upset about Faith. They sipped coffee in the dining-room speculating about what could have happened.

50 'I'm sure that the boy-friend would have taken her home by now. Most probably some teen-ager prank. They went somewhere for a cuddle in his car and then he suddenly found it couldn't start. You know the sort of thing youngsters get up to,' Miss Sophie remarked.

'I still don't understand it. Faith's not that sort of girl who would go
55 off anywhere without telling her mother,' Mary added.

'I think we are worrying for nothing. It will all end happily ever after even if Prince Charming has long sideburns and drives a red Volksie,' The Butterfly said. 'Anyone for more coffee?'

'I could do with another cup,' Mary said.

60 The Butterfly was on her way to the kitchen when there was a knock at the door.

'I'll get it,' she shouted.

'For goodness sake, no customers at this hour. We're closed till tomorrow. Tell them to go away,' Mary said urgently.

---

4 **sway**: schwanken   6 **terse**: very short, brief   21-22 **a finger supper**: light meal eaten with the fingers   24 **strike up sth.**: begin to play sth.   27 **Nou huistoe!** (Afrikaans): Back to the centre!   **inhibition**: shyness   40 **groan**: make a sound of pain   41 **Auld Lang Syne** [ɔld læŋ 'zaɪn]: Scottish song traditionally sung at the end of a party, esp. on New Year's Eve   43 **frantic**: very upset   45 **pile into sth.**: sich in etwas hineindrängen   51 **prank**: practical joke

The Butterfly stayed at the door for a long time, then returned with the empty cups still in her hands.

'I think you had better go to the door yourself,' she told Mary.

She got up wearily. At first Mary could not make out who it was whimpering in the shadows but when her eyes grew accustomed to the dark she was wide awake in an instant.

'My God, Faith, what on earth has happened to you?'

The girl was blubbering incoherently. Her dress was soiled and torn and there was a swelling above her right eyebrow.

'What has happened to you? We are all worried sick.'

'Please Aunt Mary,' Faith began, then burst out into hysterical tears.

'Come inside, my child. No-one's going to hurt you now. Butterfly, get some strong black coffee. Miss Sophie, go up and tell Mr and Mrs Knight that Faith has been found.'

Mary would not allow her to speak until her parents came hurrying in. At the same time the Globe Furnishers van drew up to report that their search was unsuccessful. Once Faith had calmed down she told her story. Elvis had plied her with more and more doctored drinks while they were sitting in his Volkswagen. She was afraid of what her mother might say so agreed to his suggestion that they go for a ride so that she could clear her head. When she found herself they were at the quarry above De Waal Drive.

'He started molesting me and tearing at my clothes. When I resisted he hit me with his fists all over my face. I managed to jump out of the car and ran all the way here. I came to Aunt Mary because I was afraid to go home.'

'I'm terribly sorry about all this,' Mary said when Faith had done.

'You're sorry?' Mrs Knight turned her anger on Mary, 'and how do you think we must feel?'

'I understand how you must feel. I also understand how this poor child must feel after such a terrible experience. It shouldn't happen to any innocent child.'

'You should be the last one to speak.'

'I think we've all had enough for one night,' her husband said, getting up and taking Faith by the arm. 'We'll have to get the child to a doctor, report to the police and then try to get some sleep. Thank you very much, Mary and all of you, for what you did.'

'There's nothing to thank about,' his wife said. 'Doesn't the same thing happen to the girls at this place? Look at the type of house you
40 run,' she resumed her attack on Mary. 'You are the one who caters for men like that monster, Elvis. You are the one who encourages people like him to do what they like to girls like Faith and get away with it. Why did my daughter have to run to you and not her mother? Answer me that.'

45 'Maybe she's afraid of her mother,' The Butterfly said quietly.

'Afraid of me? And who are you to speak? It's women like you that encourage types like that monster, Elvis.'

'Mrs Knight,' The Butterfly said steadily, 'if it wasn't for your daughter and your husband here, I would give you something to think about.
50 Now I would suggest that you shut up and say no more. You might say things you will regret afterwards. Take your daughter home. She needs a rest.'

'Yes. We've had enough excitement for one evening,' Mr Knight repeated. 'Once again thank you Mary, thank you Butterfly, thank you
55 everyone for the way you helped my child. I deeply appreciate it.'

There was an uncomfortable silence after the Knights had left.

'You know,' Zoot said, breaking it finally, 'my guardian angel is restless and suggests to me that it is now time for some follow-up action.'

'Cut the crap,' Amaai said sullenly.

60 'My guardian angel doesn't like swearing, Mr Amaai. Nor does it like any music other than hymns, as you most probably can't appreciate. It certainly doesn't like rock-'n-roll.'

'What the hell are you getting at?'

'Have any of you ever heard of a guardian angel which liked guitar
65 music and rock-'n-roll? Come on now, be honest. Guardian angels also don't like long sideburns. Maybe we should convey the message to Silvertown.'

---

4 **weary**: tired   5 **whimper**: wimmern   18 **ply sb. with sth.**: keep giving sb. large
amounts of sth.   21 **quarry**: Steinbruch   23 **molest sb.**: jdn. belästigen
40 **resume sth.**: start sth. again   **cater for sb.**: provide services for sb.
55 **appreciate sth.**: be grateful for sth.

The men all arose at the same time, went outside and climbed back into the Globe Furnishers van. Pretty-Boy directed in a pseudo-Irish accent.

'Turn left at the robot, Professor Amaai. Now turn at the second robot. Now up this street, Professor. It's in the next street, Professor Amaai.'

As they neared the house Zoot outlined the plan of action. The Jungles would park the van outside the backdoor and cover the rear while the Winsor Park boys would surround the front. They spotted the red Volkswagen parked discreetly against the side of the house. Pretty-Boy knocked loudly for some time. Eventually a light was switched on and a sixteen-year-old O'Grady girl opened the door, rubbing sleep out of her eyes.

'Hallo, beautiful.'

'Oh, it's you, Mr Pretty-Boy. Why are you visiting here at this late hour?'

'Just popping in, beautiful, just popping in.'

He heard Mrs O'Grady calling from her bedroom.

'Who's it?'

'A visitor, ma. Mr Pretty-Boy.'

'Tell him your father's in no position to see anyone, especially at this late hour.'

'I've not come to see your father, it's Elvis I'm after. He must be home now as his car's parked outside. Mind if I look?'

He forced open the door, jumped over sleeping O'Gradys and burst into Elvis's room as the latter was scrambling through the window. Pretty-Boy grabbed his electric guitar from a corner and continued in pursuit.

'It's all right,' he heard Amaai shouting from outside. 'We've got him.'

Elvis tried to brazen it out.

'I've done nothing wrong. You've got no right to burst into anyone's house like this and think you can get away with it. You've nothing on me!'

All the remaining O'Gradys except the father clustered in a frightened group at the back-door. Mrs O'Grady started screaminig.

'Would you rather rock in front of your family or in some quiet place? I would suggest we go somewhere else. Let's take him to somewhere peaceful where we won't be disturbed. What about the quarry above De Waal Drive?' Zoot suggested.

Elvis was unceremoniously flung into the back of the van, all the time professing his innocence.

'It wasn't me alone. That girl led me on. You can ask her. She said she was willing. You must believe me. Why should I lie to you?'

They dragged him out at the quarry.

'I don't suppose you can play this thing without electricity?' Zoot asked holding up the guitar. 'In any case my guardian angel does not like guitars whether electric or non-electric, so here goes.' He struck him a glancing blow with the instrument. 'And now that your pretty little guitar is broken, I'm afraid you will have to rock-'n-roll without any music. Maybe you should rock and we can roll you. When we're finished you're going to be all shook up, and you won't need any music for that. Ready for the first number, Amaai?'

They methodically set to work on him. Each one had his turn. Elvis was lying semi-conscious next to his broken guitar by the time they had finished.

'If you prefer it, we can inform the police where you are or else you can walk back to Silvertown and inform them yourself on the way,' Zoot whispered in his ear. Elvis was in no condition to hear him. The men climbed into the van and drove back to Buckingham Palace.

The following morning Mr Knight heard about it from Zoot. Later that morning his wife knocked timidly at the door of the Casbah, a plate of piping hot, just-made koeksisters in her hand. Miss Sophie answered the door.

'It's for you, Mary,' she shouted back.

---

7 **outline sth.**: etwas umreißen   8 **rear**: back   10 **discreet**: unauffällig   27-28 **in pursuit**: following   31 **brazen it out** [ˈbreɪzn]: act as if you do not feel bad about sth. even if you should   41 **unceremonious**: ohne viel Federlesens   42 **profess your innocence**: say you did not do sth.   49 **a glancing blow**: ein Schlag, der ihn streifte   64 **piping hot**: very hot

'Who's it?' Mary asked.

'It's me,' said Mrs Knight coming in. 'I want to tell you and The Butterfly and all the girls how ashamed I am about last night. No,' she said with a nervous laugh, 'I don't mean my husband, I mean about the way I behaved last evening. I was angry and relieved all at the same time, but that's no reason why I said the things I did. You must all please forgive me. You people have been very kind to my family, especially to Faith. And I want you to know that I appreciate it. I don't really know what more I can say.' She started crying softly. 'I brought you a plate of hot koeksisters. I got up early specially to fry it. You must have them now while they're hot. I think I better go now.' She put down the plate and hurried out of the door.

Mary stared at the koeksisters for a long time.

Part Three:

Night 1970

Ten years later. Five years before that, they had declared District Six a group area set aside for white occupation. Then the anger, frustration, protests and meetings. The destructive bulldozers and front-end loaders starting their punitive work, and my family embarking on its own minor diaspora.

5   *We fanned out in many directions like the spokes of a cart wheel. Finally 207, like all the other houses in Buckingham Palace, was razed to the ground without anyone consulting us. My family was luckier than most. We left before the major demolitions started. We saw the writing on the wall which could no longer be ignored. Life was becoming far too cramped and claustrophobic for*
10 *us. Everyone in the District died a little when it was pulled down. Many died spiritually and emotionally. Some like my mother also died physically although she was fortunate not to be alive to see the wholesale destruction. For her there would not be the painful memories we would experience. We buried her from 207 Caledon Street, which was still standing, and then the cortège moved*
15 *to St Mark's Church, which is now still standing. It then went by rail to Woltemade, where she was laid to rest in a cemetery set aside for our so-called ethnic group. To part is to die a little. We all died a little when we parted from the District.*

    Many were forced to move to small matchbox houses in large matchbox
20 *townships which with brutal and tactless irony were given names by the authorities such as Hanover Park and Lavender Hill to remind us of the past they had taken away from us. There was one essential difference between the old places and the new ones. District Six had a soul. Its centre held together till it was torn apart. Stained and tarnished as it was, it had a soul that held*
25 *together. The new matchbox conglomerates on the desolate Cape Flats had no soul. The houses were soulless units piled together to form a disparate community that lacked cohesion.*

---

4 **punitive**: punishing   5 **fan out**: sich fächerförmig ausbreiten   **spoke**: Speiche
6 **raze sth. to the ground**: destroy sth., demolish sth.   8 **the writing on the wall**:
warning signs   12 **wholesale**: complete   14 **cortège**: funeral procession
24 **tarnished**: (here) not perfect   26 **disparate** ['dɪspərət]: made up of very different
groups   27 **cohesion** [kəʊ'hiːʒn]: Zusammenhalt

My remaining sister married and left. Three of my brothers also married and left. One did not marry but also left. I left. None of us went in the same direction. By this time I was grown-up and qualified and went to board with a respectable, Christian family in Grassy Park who had never experienced uprooting the way I had. Although a relatively young man, I existed alone 5
with my memories in my separate cocoon in my separate area set aside for my separate group. And I tried to forget the past but the voices caught up with me and crept into the house where I was hiding, moved along the carpeted passage into the lounge with its stereophonic set and then into the kitchen with its refrigerator and electric stove and finally spilled over into my secluded bed- 10
sitting-room. And the voices whispered, 'They have done this terrible thing to you, to all of you. Go and see. They have taken your past away.'

So I went to see.

It was late one Saturday afternoon that I forced myself to go. I took the bus to Plumstead and then a train to Cape Town. I walked up to the District 15
clambering over broken bricks and half-flattened foundations of houses once inhabited by people. And the ghosts of the past swirled around me in the growing dusk. I walked along what had been Hanover Street with a few left-over houses standing self-consciously on both sides. They resembled broken teeth with craters in between where the raw gums showed. I turned up into 20
Tennant Street and then walked left along what had been Caledon Street. From that corner to St Mark's Church every building and landmark had been flattened: Handler's Drapery Store, Bernstein's Bottle Store, Buckingham Palace, Seven Steps. Only the church on Clifton Hill stood in stony defiance overlooking the destruction. I stood where the entrance to 207 had been, where 25
the house had stood in which I was born and where I had been raised. From there I could look over the desolate landscape to the dazzling lights of Cape Town which stretched to Table Bay: the neon signs, the brightly lit shops, the streetlamps whose lights failed to reach the District. In my darkening landscape individual buildings stood out in neglected silhouette: Bloemhof Flats, the 30
Zinsendorf Moravian Church, Aspeling Street Mosque and St Mark's, with the desolate winds and ghosts of the past moaning around them.

They had taken our past away and left the rubble. They had demolished our spirits and left broken bricks. They had destroyed our community and left dust and memories. And they had done all this for their own selfish and 35
arrogant reasons. They had sought to regulate our present in order to control our future. And as I stood there I was overwhelmed by the enormity of it all.

*And I asked aloud, 'What men have the moral or political right to take away
a people's past? How will they answer on that day when they have to account*
40 *for this? For the past will not be forgotten.' The south-easter swept the voices
of accusation and recrimination into all the houses into which the people had
been driven, into the matchboxes of Hanover Park and the concrete slabs of
Bonteheuwel and Manenberg. And the people on the bleak Flats whisper and
remember what greed and intolerance have done to them. And they tell their*
45 *children and their children's children because it must never be forgotten.*

*Few people were living in the few buildings and houses which still remained
on the lunar landscape. Some of those who remained were people who would
not move. Others were those who could not move.*

And then I thought of the rowdy rumbustious weekends of my childhood
50 *and my youth and compared them with these bleak weekends those who
remained are forced to endure.*

*On this Saturday of my pilgrimage, the evening lights shone bitterly in the
left-over houses, leaving tiny pin-points of isolated neglect. The south-easter
howled and wrapped itself around them as if in collusion with those other*
55 *forces bent on blowing away the last remnants of this once vibrant community.
Nobody now ventured out on Saturday evenings, because there was nowhere
to go. Star Bioscope had burnt down a few years before and the British and
National had long disappeared. There were no street-corners where youths
lounged around lamp-posts, no shops, no shebeen. Going anywhere meant*
60 *negotiating the dark, walking along bits of street and stumbling over rubble.
Hanover Street had been reduced to a broken, macadamised pathway running
nowhere over this raw and tortured landscape.*

*Sunday mornings the church bells of St Mark's still rang out defiantly,
reverberating through the empty surroundings and calling to prayer the many*
65 *who were no longer there. But the faithful heard the bells and came on foot, by*

---

5 **uproot sb.**: jdn. entwurzeln   16 **clamber**: climb   **foundation**: Fundament
20 **raw gums**: rohes Zahnfleisch   24 **defiance** [dɪˈfaɪəns]: resistance   33 **rubble**:
Geröll   39–40 **account for sth.**: explain the reasons for doing sth.
41 **recrimination**: Gegenbeschuldigung   42 **concrete slabs**: Beton   44 **greed**:
Habgier   47 **lunar**: like the moon   49 **rumbustious**: joyful, happy   51 **endure
sth.**: etwas aushalten   54 **in collusion with**: working together with   55 **remnant**:
rest   **vibrant** [ˈvaɪbrənt]: lively

bus, by train and by car. The peals reached Manenberg, Cathkin, Kensington and Retreat and people came for their weekly identification with their past. They made their ways over the rubble and stepped over the foundations of the houses they had formerly occupied. I joined in the morning service in the church which no longer had any choir stalls. The stained-glass windows 5 depicting Matthew, Mark, Luke and John were cracked and there was no organ left to boom out the accompaniment to the responses.

I remember as a boy of eight going with my mother to present our huge family bible as a gift to the church. And I now wondered whether it was still there and I was afraid to look in case it had also gone. And I also remembered 10 the brave show as the Church Lads Brigade marched up Caledon Street from their hall, with bugles blaring, drums beating and flags flying to fight the good fight. That was the one fight they could not win, and the Brigade, like other institutions, died with the District. And I also remembered how I used to sing in the church choir dressed in black cassock, white surplice and shiny, stiff and 15 scratchy Eton collar. But now the stalls were empty of boys' voices fluting, and the dwindling congregation sang ragged and unaccompanied. And after the service most of the people left to return the many miles to their Cape Flats dinners and their District Six memories.

And Sunday afternoons the same feeling of desolation settled over 20 everything. The few remaining families sought respite from their loneliness, the sameness of their lives and the ever-present threats of removal, and picked their way past Castle Bridge to bus-stops on Sir Lowry Road or made their way down to the station. And as they passed the Grand Parade they remembered the important protest meetings and the futile resolutions which 25 were passed. I myself remember marching with placards through the streets of central Cape Town as part of a long protest procession; we passed groups of whites who jeered at us. I vividly remember one man in uniform who held up his rifle in one hand and bullets in the other, and I can still see the silent contempt on his face as I wondered why he hated us. Why did he want to shoot 30 us? What made us his enemy? The south-easter gathered up my memories, my questions, my resentment and confusion and scattered them over the Flats into the houses and the concrete blocks with spidery staircases clinging to them.

And on Sunday evenings the sun set and threw the sombre landscape into deep, menacing shadow. The lights flickered on in the few remaining houses, 35 and from St Mark's came the thin, organless sounds of evensong. And then the hush of hopelessness descended and the quiet. Few children still played in the

streets and fewer made their precarious ways over the scarred land. Their
parents stayed indoors waiting for the notices to come, for the final axe to fall.
40   *And they closed their doors, shut their windows and drew down the blinds on*
their premature night and on the District that had died before its death.

---

15 **cassock**: Soutane   **surplice**: Chorhemd   16 **Eton collar**: type of high stiff collar
17 **dwindle**: get smaller   21 **seek respite (sought – sought)**: try to find peace and
quiet   28 **jeer at sb.**: jdm. höhnisch nachrufen   34 **sombre**: dark   39 **notice**:
Bescheid   40 **blinds** (pl): Jalousien

Inspector Engelbrecht

But two years before, Buckingham Palace had not yet been seriously affected.

The Boys were smoking and sunning themselves on the back-porch of Winsor Park when Pretty-Boy joined them quietly. He looked slightly older but his eyes remained as piercingly blue and innocent as ever. His hair was a thick bush of black, and women still found him attractive although he seemed impervious to any of their approaches and still had his interest only in Moena Lelik, his girl-friend of years' standing. She was still single and looked after her parents and Amaai, who was the only unmarried Jungle Boy left.

'I saw Katzen today,' Pretty-Boy said casually.

'And then you had lunch together at the Mont Nelson?' Zoot asked sarcastically.

'He says he wants to see you as soon as possible. He made it seem urgent.'

'I bet he wants money out of me. He never repairs anything in this house but always reminds us how much rent we owe him.'

Zoot also had not aged much. There was still a light spring in his step but his tap-dancing days were long over. He had also written his last, libellous poem ten years before when he was picked up for drunk and disorderly behaviour. He spent most of his time in Roeland Street playing draughts with a junior warden and when he was released he presented the policeman with a poem about his sergeant which was so accurate and scurrilous that it made the rounds of the prison offices for months afterwards. The sergeant threatened to sue for defamation but somehow never got round to it. The junior warden resigned from the force to become a bus conductor. Zoot still retained a healthy relationship with his guardian angel.

'To think how good we have been to him over all these years,' Zoot said peevishly, 'and now he wants to put us out. I have a good mind to report that skinflint.'

'To who?' Oubaas asked innocently.

'To the rent board of course, who else? That man will force me to go there and report to them that he has been overcharging us for years.'

35   'How much does he overcharge us?' Oubaas asked.

'How should I know,' Zoot replied glaring at Oubaas, 'but whatever it is, I know it is more than this place can be worth. All misers are like that, you know.'

'Yes, I suppose all misers are like that,' Oubaas agreed.

40   'So now he wants to see me. He sends his friend Pretty-Boy to tell me he wants to see me. All right then, I will go and see that Midas. But I will tell him that I am going to the rent board to complain.'

Later that afternoon Zoot strolled into Katzen's shop trying to appear casual. He fingered one or two ornaments and thought deeply as if

45 deciding what to buy. The landlord watched him warily from his desk in a corner of the shop. Katzen looked sickly and ashen. His face was pinched under a backsweep of white hair which made him look like a younger and more thick-set version of Albert Einstein.

'Shalom, my Jewish friend,' Zoot said strolling over to him. 'Peace be

50 with you and with your people.'

'Forget the nonsense,' Katzen said, annoyed, taking off his spectacles.

'But I have only come in answer to your call. When my good friend Mr Katzen calls, then who am I not to come? My guardian angel always

55 advises me to come when I am needed. Do you also have a guardian angel, my friend? But need I ask such a question? Was it not the Jews who invented guardian angels?'

'What about all the rent you owe me?'

'Now is that a fair question, Mr Katzen?'

60   'You know you have not paid me a penny for ten years.'

'Fifteen, to be exact.'

'All right, all right, fifteen years. So it's five years more. You have not paid a penny since you first moved into my house. I am becoming an old man now. My health is not good. My business is going down.

---

7 **impervious**: unempfänglich   12 **Mont Nelson**: luxury hotel   22 **draughts** [drɑːfts] (pl): Damespiel   25 **sue**: verklagen   27 **retain sth.**: keep sth. 30 **peevish**: bad-tempered   **have a good mind to do sth.**: have a strong wish to do sth.   31 **skinflint**: greedy person   41 **Midas** ['maɪdəs]: person who is able to make money easily   47 **pinched**: eingefallen

Customers are moving out of the District. So when can I expect anything from you?'

'Mr Katzen, you must believe me when I tell you the honest truth, that one day you will be most surprised. I will come into this shop with all the outstanding rent and all the interest as well. I will put it down on ⁵ this desk and I will say, "Friend Katzen, here is all your outstanding money." I will say that and then I will leave your shop and also move out of your house, and you will never see me again.'

'Yes, yes, that's all very well. But we must talk about that later. I did not send for you to talk about the rent. It was about your leaving my ₁₀ house.'

'So you are going to give us notice. Must I believe that a man whom we have always respected is now going to give us notice?'

'Mr Zoot, it is not that. It is far more serious than if I gave you notice. I have received many, many letters from the Board. Here's one of them.' ₁₅ Katzen searched among his papers and produced the document. 'Read it and you will see why I am worried.'

Zoot read slowly.

'They have been here to see me many times – a Mr Engelbrecht. I always tell him I am sick and that he must please leave me alone. It was ₂₀ a sad day for all of us when they declared the District white.'

'So what do you think they want from you?'

'They want the names of all the people who live in my houses. They want to know where they work and what they earn. They want to know what race group they belong to.' ₂₅

'And are you going to tell them, Friend Katzen?' Zoot asked, shocked out of frivolity.

'I have refused to fill in their forms up to now and I have refused to give them the information they want. But I am not well. I am not a healthy man, Mr Zoot. But I will not give in. I know how it was. I had to ₃₀ escape from Germany with just the clothes I had on. That was just before the war broke out. Did you know that?'

'No, I did not know that.'

'So now I cannot do to your people what was done to my people. Now you know. You must go. I am tired.' ₃₅

'Shalom, my friend,' Zoot said and this time he meant it seriously.

Late the following afternoon a small, officious white man in a tightly fitting navy-blue suit knocked at the door of the Casbah. The inspector had arrived in a Volkswagen bearing a government registration. In one

40 hand he clutched a bulging regulation satchel. The Butterfly answered, annoyed at being woken from her sleep.

'A bit early aren't you? You must be desperate,' she said looking him up and down.

'Better early than never,' he attempted a pun.

45 'Well, I'm sorry, we open for business after eight. You had better come back later tonight.'

'I'm afraid that's impossible. I must see someone now.'

'You really must be desperate. Well, it's up to you. But there's no-one awake except me. Everyone's asleep and I would also be sleeping if it

50 weren't for you. We must also have our rest, you know.'

He entered the house without replying and seated himself at the dining-room table.

'May I ask whether you are in charge here?'

'Lord, no. It's Mary.'

55 'Well, tell Mrs Mary that I am here to see her.'

'I'm afraid she's sleeping and it won't be very wise to wake her. But since you've woken me we might as well get on with it.'

The Butterfly had grown older over the years and it showed in the pronounced crows'-feet around her mouth and eyes. Her hair was dyed

60 a rich, flaming red. Her figure was, if anything, even more voluptuous than it had been before.

'No, I am here to speak to the head of the house.'

'Well, you can't and that's final. I'm here so let's get it over with. Like a drink as starters?'

65 'Excuse me?'

'Like a drink? The price has gone up like every bloody thing under this government.'

'I don't drink while on duty.'

---

5 **outstanding** (adj): not yet paid   13 **give sb. notice**: tell sb. to leave (a rented house or job)   27 **frivolity**: Leichtsinnigkeit   37 **officious**: übereifrig
40 **bulging**: very full   **regulation satchel**: Amtstasche   60 **voluptuous**: üppig

'Oh, my bloody hell.'

'Could I please speak to whoever is in charge?'

'Look, mister, I've told you more than once that Mary's not available. She's asleep. If you want to see her, then you must wait now or come back later tonight. I can get you a drink in the meanwhile. And you might as well buy me one also to make up for waking me.'

'Well then, maybe you can supply the information.' He took a file out of his satchel. 'What's her name?'

'Whose name?'

'The person in charge.'

The Butterfly was becoming suspicious of this unusual customer. He was behaving oddly to say the least.

'Say, mister, you're not a policeman or something, are you?'

'Certainly not. I'm from the Board. Group Areas. There's some information I must get from you people.'

'Like what?'

'Names, occupations, racial group and so on.'

'I see. So that's your game. And I thought you were a respectable customer. Now if you don't mind, mister, could you get the hell out of here? If you don't and Mary wakes up and finds you she might then knock the hell out of you. Now are you going quietly or must I help you?'

The Butterfly rose and there was an ugly look in her eyes.

'All right, all right. Tell whoever is in charge, Mrs Mary or someone, that I called. The name is Engelbrecht. Inspector Attie Engelbrecht. I'll leave these forms here. Ask her to fill them in for all of you and I'll call again tomorrow to pick them up.'

'Get the hell out of here, Mr …'

'Engelbrecht.'

'Get the hell out of here, Mr Engelbrecht, and take your bloody forms with you.'

The Butterfly slammed the door rudely behind him.

Mr Engelbrecht knocked hesitantly at the door of 203. It was jerked open and a small grizzled face grinned inanely at him. Behind the face he spotted a giant who looked idiotic.

'Good afternoon. My name is Inspector Engelbrecht. I'm from the Board.'

Oubaas continued to grin foolishly at him.

'May I come in?'

40 'I don't know?' Oubaas said.

Mr Engelbrecht entered nevertheless and sat down at a table. He withdrew the file from his satchel.

'May I ask who lives in this house?'

'All of us.'

45 'Well then, let me have your names.'

'I'm Oubaas and this here is Surprise.'

The giant extended an enormous fist and said, 'Please to meet you.' Mr Engelbrecht took it gingerly.

'Surnames?'

50 'Come again?'

'I require to know your surnames.'

'I don't think we have any, mister. And if we did have, we lost them years ago. You had better just write down Oubaas for me and Surprise for him.'

55 The giant grinned his agreement.

'And then you can also add Zoot and Pretty-Boy.'

'Occupations?'

'What?'

'What kind of work do you people do?'

60 'Where?'

'Wherever you work.'

'I don't really know.' Then Oubaas brightened. 'Maybe you should just write down businessman for me. That's right, just put down businessman.'

65 Mr Engelbrecht started to suspect that they were making a fool out of him. But that was impossible. The two looked absolutely idiotic. Or were they as stupid as they looked and sounded?

'And you?' he turned on Surprise.

---

17 **occupation**: profession, job   21 **knock the hell out of sb.**: attack sb. violently
34 **grizzled**: grey

'Assistant businessman.'

'So where do you have your businesses?'

'Oh, everywhere.'

Mr Engelbrecht was fast becoming exasperated.

'Who's in charge here?' 5

'I am,' said Zoot coming in through the back-door and sitting down opposite the inspector. The Butterfly had alerted him about the unwelcome official when he had arrived at the Casbah a few minutes earlier. He stared at Mr Engelbrecht for a long time before he spoke.

'Now who are you and what do you want?' 10

'I'm Inspector Engelbrecht. There are forms that must be completed. I need information such as your names, occupations, race groups and so on.'

'Do you mind if I ask you a question?'

'Certainly, go ahead.' 15

'Do you believe in guardian angels?'

'I'm not sure that I understand you correctly.'

'Matthew, Mark, Luke and John and that sort of thing.'

'I suppose as a Christian I do.'

'So you are a Christian. Now I have a problem. I have a guardian 20 angel, but my one is unusual. It is a non-racial guardian angel. What race does yours belong to?'

'Mr …'

'Zoot's the name.'

'Mr Zoot, I really don't know what you are getting at. I have no time 25 to waste on this sort of discussion.'

'My guardian angel would take exception to that remark. It also doesn't like people who inquire about other people's race. You must appreciate that there is nothing more unpleasant than an angry non-racial guardian angel.' 30

Mr Engelbrecht felt as if he were in a mad house. The conversation seemed to be going around in circles. Here was this man with his crazy theories about guardian angels. Another grinned toothlessly at him all the time. And a giant of an idiot crowded the door.

'If you don't mind, these forms must be filled in. You needn't do 35 them at once. I can call again tomorrow to pick them up. I'm afraid I must leave now. I still have a few more houses I must see to in this row.'

'What a pity you are in such a hurry. I was going to tell you more
40 about my non-racial guardian angel.'

'Perhaps some other time.'

The giant allowed him through. As he left, Inspector Engelbrecht heard loud and ribald laughter behind him.

A matronly woman smiled broadly when he knocked at 205. At least
45 this was a change from his hostile receptions at the two other places. She welcomed him in even before he had a chance to introduce himself properly. Her dining-room was shiny if somewhat cluttered with ornaments and other bric-à-brac. Against one wall was an expensive hi-fi set and next to it a cabinet filled with long-playing records.

50 'I'm Inspector Engelbrecht. Inspector Attie Engelbrecht.'

'Mrs Abrahams. Pleased to meet you, Inspector. Won't you please take a seat?'

'I'm sorry to bother you so late in the afternoon, but I'm from the Board. I am checking on houses in this row. There are some forms to be
55 completed. May I ask who all live here?'

'It's only my husband and myself, my daughter Moena, and my eldest son. The other two boys are married and live in Salt River.'

'Is your husband home?'

'No, he's unfortunately not here yet. He only gets in after six. My
60 daughter is also still working. But my son is home if you want to speak to him.'

'I've been given a rather bad reception at the two houses lower down from you.'

'Oh, you mustn't mind them. They don't mean harm. But they also
65 don't know how to treat white people like you. They're not used to it. Tea or coffee, Mr Engelbrecht?'

'Oh, coffee, if you don't mind.'

---

4 **exasperated** (adj): extremely annoyed   7 **alert sb.**: warn sb.   27 **take
exception to sth.**: etwas übel nehmen   43 **ribald**: rude   45 **hostile**: unfriendly,
aggressive   53 **bother sb.**: disturb sb.

'I'll just put on the water. Won't be a second. My son can speak to you in the meantime. Amaai!' she shouted into a room at the back.

A strong, morose-looking man came in. Amaai now had a thick, greying moustache. His physique was still powerful and muscular.

'Yes, can I help you?' 5

'I'm Inspector Attie Engelbrecht from the Board. I have some forms that must be filled in. Mind if I ask some questions?'

Amaai did not answer but stared hostilely. There was a long, uncomfortable pause.

'Surname and first names.' 10

'Exactly what do you want this information for, mister?'

'I believe your father is not home yet, so maybe you can help.'

'Why do you want this?'

'The Board wants it, not me. They want the names of everyone living here. The area has been declared white, as you know.' 15

'And once you have established that we are not white, you then throw us out? Is that it?'

'That's not strictly speaking correct, Mr … I didn't get your name.'

'I didn't give it.'

'Well then, I repeat what I have just said. That's not strictly speaking 20 correct.'

'Then what is strictly speaking correct?'

'We don't just throw people out. You can apply to the Council for another house in an area set aside for Coloureds.'

'What makes you think we want to move to another house in an area 25 set aside for Coloureds.'

'That's the law, mister, whether we like it nor not.'

'Whose law?'

'The country's law. You don't want to be guilty of breaking the law, do you?' 30

'Who made the law?'

'The government, I suppose.'

'Whose government?'

'I'm not here to discuss politics. I have a job to do and I'm doing it. I am supposed to get information which the Board requires. May I leave 35 these forms for your father to fill in? I can call for them tomorrow.'

'Look, mister.'

'Engelbrecht's the name.'

'I don't care a damn what your name is. Now you take your forms
40 and shove them up your backside or I'll do it for you. Now get out.'

Mrs Abrahams appeared in the kitchen doorway with a tray
containing her best tea-service and a plate of koeksisters.

'Do you realise that I can report you for this?'

'If you don't get the hell out now, you will have to report me for
45 something far more serious, if you'll be in a condition to do so.'

Mrs Abrahams knew from experience that she dared not interfere
when any of her boys were in that mood.

'So then, Mr Inspector, get out and fast!'

Mr Engelbrecht edged towards the door and then made a dash for
50 it.

Despondently he knocked at 207. No-one was at home, so he slipped
the forms in under the door. At the last house, the one nearest the
church, a greying woman opened the door and after he had mentioned
his name and the object of his call, Mrs Knight invited him inside. He
55 stayed for a very long time and, when he left to climb into his Volkswagen,
there was a satisfied smile on his face.

---

3 **morose**: bad-tempered　18 **strictly speaking**: genau genommen　23 **apply
to the Council**: beim Stadtrat einen Antrag stellen　40 **shove them up your
backside**: schieben Sie sie sich in den Hintern　49 **edge**: move slowly and carefully
49–50 **make a dash for it**: run quickly away　51 **despondent**: feeling depressed

Katzen

Two weeks after Inspector Engelbrecht's visit, everyone at Buckingham Palace received copies of the same letter from the Board. They came in official buff envelopes and some were curiously addressed. There were letters for a 'Mr Zoot', 'Miss Mary', 'Mr Amai', and one for 'The Big Man, 203 Caledon Street'. Another, addressed to the Casbah, was for 'Miss Buttercup'. The letters themselves were unambiguous and to the point. The recipients were asked to report in person to the offices in Barrack Street with proof of identity and racial group.

Zoot took his letter to Father Rowland. They had a long discussion and it was decided to call a meeting in the vestry, over which the priest would preside. Miss Sophie would be asked to send notices to all those living in Buckingham Palace as well as to Councillor Mrs Desai and Katzen. The meeting was scheduled for the Monday evening at six o'clock, by which time everyone, even those who worked, would be at home.

The vestry was crowded. Mary came early, accompanied by The Butterfly and Miss Sophie, who would act as secretary. Moena Mooies was asked to stay at home and stave off potential customers. The Winsor Park Boys arrived slightly earlier, as Surprise was to act as doorman. Then Mr and Mrs Abrahams came with Amaai and Moena Lelik. The latter smiled when she saw Pretty-Boy, and went to sit next to him. They were still very much in love. Mr and Mrs Knight and their remaining daughter, Charity, came last. Faith had married a teacher and, as her mother used to announce to everyone who cared to listen, was now living in her own house in Retreat. Hope was in Johannesburg, an apostle and choir-leader in her uncle's church.

Father Rowland opened the proceedings with a short prayer. Then Miss Sophie read a letter just received from Councillor Mrs Desai, in which she apologised for her absence and pledged solidarity with them. She urged all to stand together. 'There are thousands more like you who are also threatened by this pernicious Act. If we all stand firm they cannot move us easily. If one of us gives in it will make it harder for everyone else. So remember that united we stand, divided we must

surely fall.' Miss Sophie then read out a copy of the official letter they
35 had all received from the Board.

Father Rowland clarified the legal position. He explained that, as
they all knew, parts of District Six had been declared white three years
before in 1965. Theirs was one part. Those who remained and were not
white, like everyone present in the vestry, were designated by Pretoria as
40 disqualified persons. They could therefore be forced to move to a group
area for which they were qualified by law.

Zoot asked whether this applied to everyone.

'No. The best areas are kept for whites. No single white family I know
of has been forced to move under the Act. If there are any families there
45 must be very few.'

'So then what do we do about these letters? Do we simply go to
Barrack Street as requested?' Zoot asked again.

'No, you need not go unless you choose to do so. This letter *requests*
you to go. There is nothing in it which compels you. It is merely a
50 request to present yourselves. You thus have the right to ignore it as you
could any other request.'

'And what about the information they require?'

'You can ignore that as well. Don't give anyone any information
unless you are forced by Pretoria to do so. And if they do apply official
55 pressure, then see a lawyer first.'

'And let's say, for argument's sake, they have compelled us to give
them the information and they now have proof that we are disqualified
persons, how long can we still remain here?'

'Let's get the facts straight. Firstly they must establish that you live
60 here. That's easy enough. Then they must have proof of your race group.
This they can do only if you co-operate with them and present yourselves.
Thirdly they must be able to show that you are not qualified to live
here.'

'And then?'

---

3 **buff**: yellowish, brown   6 **unambiguous**: absolutely clear   11 **preside**: be the
chairman   18 **stave off sb.**: jdn. zurückweisen   20–21 **the latter**: the last one
named   29 **pledge sth.**: promise sth. firmly   31 **pernicious**: evil and cruel
act: law   49 **compel sb.**: force sb.   **merely**: only   56 **for argument's sake**:
theoretically

'Then Pretoria can force you to sign an agreement that you will vacate the premises. It might not even be necessary for them to do that.'

'And then?'

'Then they have the legal right to put you out. But they must give you at least three months' notice.' 5

There was hopeless silence.

'May I say something?' Oubaas asked breaking the long pause.

'Certainly.'

'I am not a clever man. I know that. I haven't got any education. I know that also. I was never even a master painter as I lied to Pretty-Boy 10 years ago. But there is something that worries me and that I can't seem to work out for myself. Who is this Pretoria you are always speaking about? Pretoria says this and Pretoria says that. Pretoria says we must give our names and our race. Pretoria says we must report to that office in Barrack Street. Now, someone tell me, who then is Pretoria? What 15 right has Pretoria to do what it does. Can anyone here answer me?' There were tears of anger and frustration in his otherwise mild eyes.

Zoot listened in amazement to this unexpected outburst. 'Pretoria is trouble,' he said laconically.

Father Rowland got discussion going. Mrs Knight asked to speak. 20

'Isn't it better if we all just go to the Board and ask the officials to give us other houses? They will see that we are decent people and will surely place us in a decent area. Otherwise, before we know it, we might be out on the streets with nowhere to go. And what do we do then?'

'We don't go anywhere. We stay right here and we all stay here 25 together,' The Butterfly said fiercely.

'It's all very well for you to speak. You only have yourself to think of. You have no-one else to worry about. I have a family. My husband is not at all well and his business is dropping. And Charity here is still a pupil at Trafalgar in matric. So where do you expect decent people like us to 30 go if they put us out?'

'You can go and live with your daughter in Retreat,' her husband muttered angrily, 'or better still, go to your other daughter and her fake uncle in Johannesburg. But for goodness sake leave me out of it.' He looked ill and the effort made him shiver and his eyes water. 35

'It is very important that we stand together. If one of us goes now, all of us will have to go eventually. So I agree with The Butterfly that we must stay,' Pretty-Boy said.

'We will all have to go eventually whether we like it or not,' Mrs
40 Knight persisted. 'We mustn't meddle in politics. That's not our business. We cannot fight the government and hope to win. I say that if we have to go sooner or later, we might as well go sooner than later.'

'We don't have to go either sooner or later until they force us. I propose that we all stay here,' Pretty-Boy said.

45 Father Rowland was trying to bring some measure of accord between the opposing members when a soft knock was heard at the door. Surprise looked out.

'It's someone who came by taxi.'

'Oh dear, I hope it's not a customer,' Mary said. 'Now why on earth
50 did Moena have to tell them where we were? Butterfly, explain to whoever it is that we're busy now.'

A heavily muffled man entered before The Butterfly could get up. Although it was a mild evening, he was wrapped in an overcoat and scarf.

55 'May I join the meeting, please?'

He took off his astrakhan hat.

'Good heavens, it's Katzen,' Zoot said. 'Of course you may join us. Let me get you a chair.'

Katzen looked pale and drawn and did not remove his coat and scarf.
60 For a moment his body was racked with coughs.

'I am not at all well, as you can see,' he said apologetically, 'but I felt it was my duty to come. I got out of bed specially.'

1–2 **vacate the premises**: leave the house   5 **three months' notice**: dreimonatige Kündigungsfrist   34 **for goodness sake**: um Himmels Willen   40 **meddle in sth.**: interfere in sth.   45 **some measure of accord**: some agreement   52 **heavily muffled**: schwer eingemummt   59 **pale**: white   **drawn**: ill-looking   60 **racked with coughs**: shaking due to his coughing

'You are most welcome,' Father Rowland began, 'but shouldn't you rather be back in your bed? We appreciate your coming but I think it is best if I phone a taxi for you.'

'No, no, no. I want to be here. I must be here. It is my duty. Besides there is something I must tell you all.'   5

'I don't think it wise for you to exert yourself on our behalf.'

'I will be all right. If I could have a glass of water, please.'

'We deeply appreciate your concern and sacrifice,' Father Rowland said.

'It is not much of a sacrifice, but I do have great concern for all of   10
you, for all of us, that's why I am here. I want to explain to you why I came. You must bear with me. I am a sickly and talkative man. Have I your permission to continue?'

'Please continue and stop whenever you feel you cannot go on.'

'Well then, where must I begin? You all know me simply as Katzen,   15
that stingy Jew Katzen who has a shop in Hanover Street and is always wanting rent from you. But my full name is Solomon Katzen. It is as Solly that I was always known when I grew up in a little village of Veckerhagen in Germany. It is in Brunswick on the River Weser. You know it? *Die Schöne Weser*. I was born there before the start of the First   20
World War. My father was a poor struggling rabbi with a tiny congregation. You see we were very few Jews in the village and we did not even have a proper synagogue. I went to the volksschule in Gieselwerder, a few miles away. It was not too bad there although the other schoolchildren sometimes called us "dirty Jews" and "Christ killers". Yes, of course it hurt me a lot but I had learnt early already not   25
to show it, even when they spat on me. Then when I was twenty I was sent by my parents to the university in Hanover to study to become a lawyer. They were poor, as I said, but they had great ambitions for me, their only son. In spite of the persecution I had done well at school and my father always used to say, "Solly, be proud of being a Jew. Jews have   30
brains. You are Jewish and you have brains. Show the *goyim* what a Jewish boy can do." They used up all their savings to send me to university.'

Everyone was listening intently. It had never struck them that Katzen had a past, had any name other than Katzen, was a German and had   35
been a law student at a university. For them he had always been just

Katzen, a figure of ridicule in his food-stained black suit which he always wore, his unshapely boots, his thick walrus moustache, his wild white hair and his ragged beard. He had always been considered an anomaly
40 in District Six, someone who was taken for granted but did not really belong.

'Then in 1932 Adolf Hitler became Chancellor of Germany and our lives as Jews became very difficult. There were very few of us still at university, and for the rest I had only one gentile friend, Dieter Reinecke,
45 who was also a law student. We used to go for long walks along the banks of the Weser, Dieter and I, past the pretty, little village of Halzminden and Rühle to Hameln. All the other gentiles at the university avoided me and even tried to persuade Dieter to do so. When they did not succeed they spread the rumour that he was half-Jewish.' Katzen
50 paused to sip some water. 'My health is bad now but my memory is still good.

'At first they used force to exclude us from the universities and professions. But when that was not sufficiently effective, they passed laws. Why is it that the more frightened people become the more laws
55 they pass? Confident people do not need to pass so many laws. You have heard of Nürnberg? How do you say it in English? The Nuremberg Laws. Those laws took away our citizenship or what was left of it. We became *staatsangehörige* – subject people, people who did not have the vote, people who did not have any say in the government.'
60 '*Staatsangehörige*,' Zoot repeated softly.

Katzen had another bout of coughing and smiled apologetically as he wiped his lips.

6 **exert yourself**: sich anstrengen   31 **goyim** (Yiddish): non-Jewish people
34 **it had never struck them that …**: they had never thought about the fact that …
38 **unshapely**: worn out, in a bad condition   39 **anomaly**: sb./sth. different
from the rest   40 **take sb./sth. for granted**: expect sb./sth. always to be there
44 **gentile**: non-Jewish   49 **spread a rumour**: ein Gerücht verbreiten
52 **exclude sb.**: shut sb. out   58 **staatsangehörige**: while non-Jewish Germans
became 'Reichsbürger' under the Nuremberg Racial Laws, Jews were given the status
of 'Staatsangehörige'   61 **bout of coughing** [baʊt]: Hustenanfall

'But I am afraid that I am taking up too much of your time. You must have more important things to talk about and have not the time to waste on my rambling story. So maybe I should stop now and go home.'

'Please go on,' Mary said gently.

'All right then. Now where was I? Oh yes. We could not vote. We could not marry gentiles. There was a law which said it was immoral and illegal for us to do so. It was called "The Law for the Protection of German Blood and German Honour". If we married a gentile then we broke the law. We had no say in making the laws. Nobody consulted us about the laws which governed us. You understand?'

Zoot nodded his agreement.

'I had left the university long before I could get my degree. It was better so. The professors and students made life difficult for us. Those who could get away left Germany. My father's oldest brother managed to get to your country, to Johannesburg. He urged us to join him. My parents desperately wanted me to follow him. They said I was young and strong and could start a new life in a new country. They could not force themselves to leave although the situation was getting unbearable for them. You see, they could only see themselves as Germans and loved Germany in spite of the way if was treating them.

'I was determined not to leave and did whatever work I could find. I was a porter at the railway station in Löhne, I sold newspapers, I packed crates in a shop in Holzminden. Anything to get a few marks to keep us alive. We were banned from schools, from universities and professions. They regarded us as *untermenschen* – sub-humans.

'Then came the Night of the Broken Glass – the *Reichskristallnacht*. A Jew in Paris, so they said, shot and killed a junior secretary at the German Embassy. They used that as a pretext to unleash the most terrible pogroms. My parents were arrested with thousands of other Jews throughout Germany. At first my mother and father were sent to Natweiler Concentration Camp but afterwards they were gassed in Auschwitz. I hid for a short time with Dieter's family and then managed to escape to Holland, from where I was smuggled to England. I heard long afterwards that Dieter also died at Auschwitz. During the war I worked for British Intelligence as an interpreter. Maybe that's why I speak English so good and had all those pictures of King George the Sixth, remember?'

Katzen again smiled apologetically and shrugged his shoulders. No-one broke the silence which followed until he spoke again.

40 'It is very funny for me. In Germany they treated me as an *untermenschen*. Here they force me to be part of the *herrenvolk*. But I cannot forget what they did to us in Germany. So my heart is with all the *untermenschen*, whoever and wherever they are.'

He paused briefly to sip more water.

45 'Oh yes and this is what I must say. I almost forgot. They tell me that if I want to sell my houses in the District, I can only sell them to white people. If I want to sell my business, I can only sell it to white people. If anyone moves out of any of my houses, only white people can move in. So I have decided that while this evil law remains I will never sell my 50 houses. I will never sell my business. If any of you move out, the houses will stand empty. And I will also not give them any information. I will not fill in any of their forms. You must believe me when I say so.'

'We do believe you, Mr Katzen. All of us believe you,' Zoot said quietly.

55 'So now I must go. I have spoken too long and spoken too much. I must thank you also for listening to me. Can someone please phone for a taxi?'

'My car is parked outside,' Amaai said slowly. 'I would consider it a great honour if I could drive you home.'

60 For a long time after Katzen had left the rest of the meeting sat in silence. It grew darker but no-one moved to switch on the lights. Each sat wrapped in his or her own thoughts. Then, without saying a word they got up and went back to their homes in silence.

9 **have no say in sth.**: not be involved in sth.   28 **pretext** ['priːtekst]: Vorwand
unleash sth.: etwas entfesseln

The Last of the Knights

Mary was most surprised one Tuesday afternoon two months later, when The Butterfly woke her from her usual nap to report that Charity, the youngest daughter of the Knights, was at the front door. The girl, who was now in Senior Certificate at Trafalgar High, was still in school uniform. Her presence was unusual as it was common knowledge that Mrs Knight discouraged any form of contact between her children and what she termed 'those girls at the Casbah'.

'Good afternoon,' she greeted The Butterfly, 'is my Aunty at home?'

'Oh, it's Charity. Yes, of course. She has just woken up. Step inside while I tell her you're here.'

'I hope it's all right,' Charity said more to herself than to The Butterfly.

'Of course it's all right. Come on in.'

Mary was very curious about the visit and soon entered the dining-room.

'Afternoon, Aunt Mary.'

'Afternoon, Charity. What a welcome surprise. My but you have grown into a beautiful lady. And with brains as well. To what do I owe this pleasure?'

There was obviously something bothering the girl and she seemed to have difficulty continuing.

'Is something the matter?' Mary's tone was worried.

'Well, yes, Aunty. Mother has sent me with a message that she would like to come over to see you later this afternoon, about five o'clock if that's convenient for you. She said to tell you it was important.'

'What can be so important? Is something bothering you, my child?'

Charity could not hold back her tears any longer and cried quietly. Mary gently lowered her into a chair and sent The Butterfly to make some strong black coffee.

Once they were alone Mary said gently, 'You can tell me what is wrong, but only if you wish to.'

'Aunty, we are moving out this evening.'

'Where to, my girl?'

'Hanover Park. Mother had accepted a council flat for us in a block
35 called Azalea Court. I haven't been there yet and don't even know where
Hanover Park is. Pa won't speak about it. I think Mother's the only one
enthusiastic about going.'

'How long have you all known about this?'

'I'm not sure. I know she started talking about it well before the
40 meeting you people had in the church. Mother went to the Board's office
in Cape Town soon after that Inspector came round. Aunty, I don't want
to move.'

'You must go wherever your family goes. You're the only daughter
they have left. They depend on you. District Six is no longer a good
45 place in which a young girl can grow up.'

'But you grew up here,' she said reproachfully.

'That was a long, long time ago and things weren't so bad then. Also
it's not entirely true to say that I grew up here. I came from the Boland
when I was slightly younger than you are now. Yes, maybe I will soon
50 have to go back to the mission station to look after my father. Maybe I
will also be going. The District is no longer a good place. It is filthy and
squalid and with people moving out there are too many derelict houses
inhabited by too many skollies. None of us knows how long we will still
be allowed to remain here. District Six is falling apart, Charity, and a
55 pretty and clever girl like you should know better than to remain in a
place that is falling apart.'

'I don't care if it is falling apart. I like it here. I understand it. I don't
want to live in Hanover Park. Neither does Pa, but he's not a strong man
and does what Mother tells him to do.'

60 'Did your mother mention what she wanted to see me about?'

'No, Aunty, but I think it's because she feels guilty. She doesn't want
to show it but she's worried that people will accuse us of deserting, of
leaving them in the lurch. I think she's coming to try to make her peace.
You must refuse to see her, Aunty.'

---

4 **Senior Certificate**: class in which students prepare themselves for their school-
leaving exams   17 **my**: expression of surprise   34 **council flat**: Sozialwohnung
46 **reproachful**: critical   52 **squalid**: poor and unpleasant   **derelict**: verlassen und
verfallen   63 **leave sb. in the lurch**: leave sb. who needs help

'You are being unfair, my girl. I'm sure your mother is doing her best for you and your father.'

The Butterfly came in with the coffee.

'Now stop crying and have some of this. It will do you good.'

Mary changed the subject and asked her questions about her school, what she hoped to do afterwards, the college she wished to enter, her sister Faith, who was now Mrs Faith Arendse and living in her own house in Retreat.

'Thank you, I'm feeling much better now. I think I had better go. I don't know when I'll see you people again, but I'll try to drop in some of the afternoons after school, if that's all right with you.'

'Of course it will be all right with us.'

'Thank you for the coffee, Butterfly and Aunty, goodbye for now. Goodbye, Butterfly.'

'Goodbye, my girl and good luck. Tell your mother that I'll be home at five.'

Mrs Knight arrived promptly. She was bearing a large tin of home-made biscuits. Mary was sitting in the dining-room with The Butterfly. The atmosphere was cordial and strained. After some preliminary remarks, Mary asked, 'Tea or coffee?'

'Tea, please, if you don't mind. And I've brought along some biscuits I've just made.'

'Thank you but I mustn't eat too much of the stuff. Sweet things don't agree with me.'

'I'm sure these won't harm you.'

Mary sent The Butterfly to prepare the refreshments in the kitchen. Looking hard at Mrs Knight she came straight to the point.

'I believe you are moving out this evening.'

'Yes, so in a way I'm coming to say *tot siens*.'

'I'm very sorry that you're going.'

For a moment no-one spoke.

'We had no real choice in the matter. We were very lucky to get a flat so soon. I had to take it. The waiting list is five years long.'

'I believe so. I know many people who have been waiting longer. Everyone is desperate for houses and flats in the townships.'

'I went in to see the Board soon after Inspector Engelbrecht suggested it. Didn't he tell you people the same thing?'

'Yes, but we ignored it,' The Butterfly said coming in with the tray.

40 'They asked for our identity documents. Then they made my husband sign an agreement that we would vacate our house within two months. Joseph was unwilling to do so but I persuaded him, since it was only then that we could be considered for another place.'

The Butterfly stood listening at the kitchen door with the tray still in
45 her hands. Mary made no comment.

'They won't even start considering you for another house unless you sign an agreement to vacate the present one. But I made them promise to give us one in a decent neighbourhood amongst decent people like ourselves. They promised me that they would.'

50 'You going to Hanover Park?'

'Yes. It's not too bad. We've been given a small two-roomed flat on the second floor of a block called Azalea Court. The rent is a bit high but the place suits us since there are only the three of us left.'

'So you plan to leave tonight?' The Butterfly asked.

55 'Yes.'

'Is it not too late to change your mind?' she asked.

'We can't really do so now.'

'Tell me,' The Butterfly continued, putting down the tray with more force than was necessary, 'why did you people decide to leave?'

60 'Because we had no alternative.'

'Neither have we but we are still here.'

'What the government says in this country is law. What they want, they take.'

'Have you considered the consequences of your actions?' The
65 Butterfly asked coldly.

'What consequences can be worse than remaining?'

'Have you thought what effect moving will have on the rest of your family?'

'Of course I have.'

17 **bear sth.**: carry sth.   21 **cordial**: polite and friendly   29 **tot siens** [tɒt siːnz] (Afrikaans): goodbye

Mary took up the argument. 'Do you realise that you are moving to an area you don't even know? Here you were surrounded by familiar things. You lived amongst us. We formed a community. We were always together as one. We knew one another. Who do you know out there?'

'We can always make new friends. That shouldn't be too difficult. We 5 had to make new friends when we first came here, didn't we? One place is much like another. One community is much like another.'

'There you are wrong,' Mary said. 'One place might be like another, but one community is never like another. A community is not just a place where you live. It is not just another locality like Hanover Park or 10 Bonteheuwel. It is much more than that. It is alive. A community is our home. It is the place where many of us were born and spent most of our lives. It is a place where, before this wicked law was passed, most of us also hoped to die. It is a place some of us come home to rest in after a heavy day's work, to be with friends and neighbours. It is a place of 15 warmth, of friendship, of love and of quarrels. Here we enjoy a feeling of togetherness. Will you find that in Hanover Park? Can you build up a community overnight?'

'I'm only doing what I think is best for my family,' Mrs Knight defended herself. 'All of us will have to leave eventually. The only 20 difference is that we are going now and you will go later. One cannot fight this government.'

'But one can fight one's selfishness. One can fight the temptation to think only of oneself and one's family. Yes, maybe you're right. May be we all have to go later. But that later could come sooner because people 25 like you are going now.'

'You are not being fair. My husband and daughter mean everything to me. Joseph is not well but he won't lift a finger even when he is. So I must act for the family. And when I do, I get criticised for it. I am keeping a roof over our heads.' 30

'You have one here.'

'For how long, if I may ask?' Mrs Knight was near to tears. She got up very hesitantly. 'I'm sorry if I've taken up your time. I think I had better leave now. We still have lots of packing to do. The lorry is coming at eight this evening. Well then, I won't say goodbye, only *tot siens*.' 35

The Butterfly turned on her heel and walked out.

'*Tot siens*,' Mary said softly, 'and don't think I don't understand, because I do.' Then she added, 'If ever you need us and we're still here, we'll come. Don't be afraid to ask. We will always remain one community
40 no matter how they try to force us apart.'

Mrs Knight walked out quickly holding a handkerchief to her eyes. For a long time Mary sat staring at the cups of tea and plate of biscuits which no-one had touched.

Zoot reported the following day that 209 was now standing empty.
45 He also added that Last-Knight's shop in Tennant Street had a notice in the window that it would be closed for the next three days.

A month later Zoot passed the barber's shop. Since it was still early it was empty of customers and Last-Knight was sitting alone on a chair in the corner reading that day's copy of the *Cape Times*.
50 'Morning,' Zoot said, entering. 'Since when have you been back?'

Last-Knight lowered his newspaper, and Zoot was amazed at his physical transformation. He was now thin and haggard, his skin ashen and loose, and his hair grey and untidy.

'Morning,' he answered slowly.
55 'When did the shop reopen?'

'It was only shut for a few days when we moved. I have been here since. Can I help you?'

'No, I have not come for the pleasure of a haircut and shave, my tonsorial friend. I have only come to meet an old acquaintance who
60 should not be forgotten.'

'That is very kind of you. I was starting to believe that all you people were against me.'

'So how are things in Hanover Park?'

'We no longer live there.'
65 'Really?'

'We are now staying in a room at the back of Faith's house in Retreat.'

---

23 **selfishness**: thinking of oneself first   52 **haggard**: looking tired and ill   **ashen**: grey

'Could you not pay the rent or something like that and did the Council put you out? Now that was extremely foolish of you,' Zoot began flippantly, but when he saw the hurt expression on Last-Knight's face he changed his tone immediately.

'I'm sorry, I was just being silly. Forget it. As you were saying?' 5

'The three weeks in Hanover Park were an experience I would not like to go through again. Finally we couldn't take it any longer. I blame myself entirely for allowing my wife to get us into such a predicament.'

'Why did you agree to go in the first place? Nobody was forcing you? You could have waited a bit longer.' 10

'Yes, I see now that we could. But I was weak and tired. I left everything to my wife, all the decisions, which was unfair of me. I merely signed the forms. Up to the night we moved I didn't have any desire or guts to see the new flat. And once I saw it, I knew we had made a terrible mistake.' 15

'What did you see?'

'The flats were all in a bad state of disrepair although they were only two years old. Our one, like the others in Azalea Court, had no ceiling. The lights had been disconnected and not been reconnected. The first few nights we spent in the cold and the dark. The place was damp and 20 smelt of mildew. There were draughts in every room. The walls were full of cracks.'

'That must have been most unpleasant. Now my guardian angel would have …'

'Excuse me?' 25

'No, nothing. I was only being silly again.'

'There was no post-office nearby such as we had in Hanover Street. The nearest postbox was in the town centre, which was quite a distance from us. There were no private phones; the only public one was in the post office, and out of order. No neighbourhood shops like Moodley 30 and Baptiste or the hawkers here who come round with carts full of fruit and vegetables. We were completely cut off. There was nothing but filth and sand and rows and rows of washing-lines.'

Zoot noticed that Last-Knight's hands were shivering as he spoke.

'We felt completely isolated. To get here to my shop meant extra 35 petrol. I gave Charity a lift to school in the mornings but in the afternoons she had to wait for me at the shop until I finished after six, or else she

had to take a train to Claremont, a bus to Hanover Park and then she still had a long and dangerous walk to Azalea Court. One afternoon,
40 three days after we had moved in, some skollies interfered with her and tore at her clothes. The child was so frightened that she ran all the way home, leaving her satchel behind. She lost all her schoolbooks. She was hysterical when she got to the flat. After that she never went anywhere on her own and besides dropping her in the morning I had to fetch her
45 at school in the afternoon. She would sit here doing her homework until I was ready to leave. Sometimes I finished the last customer well after eight o'clock.'

'District Six is no longer safe either.'

'I suppose so, but over the years we have learned to know everyone
50 and everyone has learned to know us. No-one would dream of harming any of the children here. We were all neighbours and we all enjoyed a spirit of neighbourliness. In Hanover Park there is nothing like that and I feel there never will be. Each family lives for itself. We felt as if we had no roots, as if we were living in a transparent bowl suspended somewhere
55 on the second floor of Azalea Court. '

'Weren't you expecting too much?'

'No, I don't think so. We were expecting what we were used to. Poor and dilapidated as Buckingham Palace is, we could sit on our front stoep at night and see the outlines of Table Mountain, Lion's Head and Signal
60 Hill. We could sit on the back porch and see the ships at anchor in Table Bay. We could see the lights shining right down to the docks. Where we were living in Azalea Court, when we opened the front door we could see only washing-lines and more washing-lines and the opposite courts.'

65 'I understand.'

'In spite of all that we decided to make a go of it. One morning during the second week all the tyres of my car were slashed. It was parked in the court. Then the third week-end we had warnings that we

---

3 **flippant**: not serious, joking   8 **predicament**: difficult situation   14 **guts** (infml): courage   21 **mildew** ['mɪldjuː]: Mehltau   54 **bowl**: Schüssel   **suspend sth.**: hang sth.   58 **dilapidated**: in a very bad state   66 **make a go of it**: try to make the best of sth

could expect trouble. I took Charity to stay with Faith in Retreat. At three in the morning a gang burst into our flat looking for her. They smashed all the furniture and took the radio set and tape recorder. It was then that we decided we had had enough. We moved out the same day without bothering to give notice. Now we are all cramped up in one room in Retreat.' 5

'You must have been through hell.'

'How can they do this to us? Why did the government not just leave us alone? We left only because they told us how insecure it would be if we stayed on here. They did not tell us how insecure it would be if we went there. We were afraid of being put out onto the streets. That Mr Engelbrecht promised us the earth. So we went, and look what happened. What would have happened to my daughter if she had been at home? We couldn't go through all that again.' 10

Tears were streaming down his face while he tried ineffectually to wipe his eyes. He looked even older and more helpless. 15

'I am too sickly to start my life all over again. Maybe if they had left us alone in the District it would have been better.'

'Maybe,' Zoot repeated.

He got up and left the shop. He could not bear to see a grown man crying. 20

The Abrahamses

Every Monday and Thursday evening at 5.30 p.m. Pretty-Boy waited for his girlfriend Moena at the Hanover Street bus-stop next to the Fish Market. She had been a seamstress at Robinson's in Glynn Street for the
25   past few years and usually took the bus from Darling Street. They would then either walk up Clifton Hill and then down into Caledon Street or alternatively climb up Seven Steps past Ayre Street and then turn left to get to her house in Buckingham Palace.

That Thursday when Pretty-Boy met her as usual, Moena looked
30   worried and suggested that they go for a walk first as she had things on her mind she wished to speak about. They strolled up Clifton Hill past St Mark's Church. Along the way they passed many houses now empty and derelict. It was obvious that the stream of people leaving the District was gathering momentum and that few were moving in. They reached
35   Upper Constitution Street and then cut across a few fields to get to De Waal Drive. After negotiating the heavy stream of traffic moving in both directions, they were finally on the mountain-slope and followed a contour footpath through the pine forest. It was getting darker and, below, the lights of Cape Town were twinkling into life.

40   They had been discussing ordinary matters quietly until they sat down to rest on a rocky outcrop.

'There's something I have been meaning to tell you for some time now, Pretty-Boy.'

'What is it, my dear?'

45   'I don't know how to begin. All right then. We're moving out of the District tomorrow.'

Far away they could barely make out the sounds of traffic chasing homewards. Around them settled the silence of the plantation.

Pretty-Boy reprimanded her gently. 'But why did you not tell me
50   before?'

---

15 **ineffectual**: without result   24 **seamstress**: clothesmaker   34 **gather momentum**: get faster/bigger   36 **negotiate sth.**: (here) move through sth. carefully
41 **rocky outcrop**: vorragender Felsen

'I was afraid.'

'Afraid of me?'

'Yes, and of everyone else. I was afraid of what people would say about our deserting like this.'

'You believe then that you are deserting?' 5

'Yes, I do.'

'Where are you moving to?'

'Mother's found a large semi-detached cottage in Rose Street. It's the same street in Schotsche Kloof where we lived before.'

'Then I'm very happy for you.' 10

'It does make it easier. It helps because it is in a group area set aside for so-called Cape Malays. Apparently we qualify. Mother had been at the Council for the past month.'

'So you knew for some time?'

'I knew we were moving, but I only learnt on Tuesday, two days ago, 15 when exactly it would be. No-one speaks about it at home except mother, who speaks about it all the time.'

'And your father?'

'He does what mother tells him to do. She did all the negotiation. He signed all the forms.' 20

'And Amaai?'

'There was a big row when he found out about the moving. Lately he hasn't spoken to anyone in the house except me. He gets up in the morning, washes, eats and drives off to work without a word to anyone. At night he listens to his records for hours after we have all gone to bed. 25 I saw him this morning but was afraid to tell him. There is something terrible boiling up inside him. I'm frightened for him. Pretty-Boy, I'm frightened of him.'

'Does he know about your going tomorrow?'

'No, but I know he realises that it could be any day now.' 30

'Then there'll be trouble when he gets home and finds you're all gone?'

'Yes, there'll be lots of trouble. I only hope he won't take it so badly that he won't come and live with us and go somewhere else.'

'And you?'

A thin mist was spreading round them and down into the city, and 35 the air on the slope was suddenly chilly. Moena shivered slightly but whether from the cold or fear of the situation it was hard to tell.

'Shall we go back?' Pretty-Boy suggested.

'Yes, I think so.'

40 They got up and started walking, with the fallen leaves and dried twigs crunching underfoot.

'And you? How do you feel about it all, Moena?'

'I don't want to leave, Pretty-Boy, it's true, I don't want to leave.'

He put his arms around her to guide her in the growing dark.

45 'I don't want to leave the District. I don't want to leave you.'

They were on De Waal Drive now waiting for a break in the traffic in order to cross over.

'What can I do, Pretty-Boy?'

He paused and then shouted above the roar of the cars speeding by.

50 'You can marry me!'

He rushed her skilfully over the drive.

'Did you hear me?' he asked, a bit more subdued now that they were on the other side.

'Yes, I heard you.'

55 ''So?'

'No, Pretty-Boy, that will be impossible.'

'But why, Moena?'

'I cannot marry anyone while my parents are still alive. They are getting older and need someone to look after them. They depend on me.'

60 'But there's Amaai also.'

'No, they need their daughter to look after them. It is my duty. Father is talking of retiring as soon as we move. One never knows when Amaai might leave home. He might do so tomorrow when he finds out. He could get married like Toyer and Braima. Then there's only my income, 65 little as it is.'

'But it's unfair to place such a burden on yourself.'

'No, it's my duty.'

'Has the fact that I am a Christian anything to do with it?'

'No, it hasn't, although, fond as they are of you, I know it would hurt 70 my parents if I did not marry a Muslim.'

---

36 **slope**: hillside   **chilly**: unpleasantly cool   41 **crunch**: make the noise of being trampled, crushed and broken   52 **subdued**: gedämpft   66 **burden**: Last
69 **fond as they are**: so lieb sie dich auch haben

'I'm prepared to change my religion.'

'It's no use, Pretty-Boy. My hands are tied while they need me. But we can remain close, can't we? You must promise to visit me in Rose Street.'

'I promise, and I also promise to wait for you until you can marry me.'

They were walking down past Milton Street and were now in Richmond Street. On either side were more derelict houses. Rubble and broken bricks were scattered everywhere.

They reached 205 and stood quietly on the stoep. Next to the church the Knights' house was ghost-like and forlorn. The adjacent house, 207, had long been empty. The family had moved out after their mother had died. Finally there were only two of them left, the eldest and youngest boys. The eldest moved to live with his married sister in Kensington, and the youngest, after qualifying as a teacher, went to board in Grassy Park. Two of Katzen's houses stood lonely and deserted waiting for the third to join them the following day. True to his word he allowed no-one to move in.

'What time do you move tomorrow?'

'The lorry will be here at ten. We must have everything shifted before Amaai gets home at five. I only hope he doesn't take it too badly. I'm staying home to help tomorrow.'

'Well, I suppose I'll see you in the morning. Good night, Moena.'

'Good night, Pretty-Boy.'

The following day The Boys were already sunning themselves on their stoep when the removal lorry arrived. The driver had one labourer to help. Moena was supervising the packing.

'So they are also leaving,' Zoot said bitterly.

Pretty-Boy, at whom the question was directed, made no reply.

'Did you know about it?'

He could not avoid the direct question. 'Yes, I knew about it.'

'For some time now?'

'No, I only knew for certain last night.'

'Moena told you?'

'Yes.'

They were silent. Their periods of silence were growing longer lately. At last Oubaas got up, stretched himself and asked sheepishly, 'Anyone for a drink?' No-one replied. He went inside and returned with an unopened five-litre can of wine. Where he could have found or stored
40 it, nobody could guess. He could certainly not afford to buy it. He had glasses with him and poured out wine all round.

'Does Amaai know about this?' Zoot asked Pretty-Boy.

'Yes, but he doesn't know it is today.'

'So when he comes home they'll be gone and there'll be hell to pay.
45 Does he know where they are going to?'

'I suppose he must.'

The driver and labourer were struggling ineffectually to manoeuvre a large wardrobe through the door. Moena tried to direct them. The men were sweating with the exertion.
50 'I think I should help,' Surprise said, getting up.

'No,' Zoot said fiercely. 'Sit down. No-one of us helps. If they want to move let them do so on their own.'

Pretty-Boy drained his glass and without a word walked over to assist. This was open defiance. Up to now he had never seriously
55 challenged Zoot's decisions. They had quarrelled often enough and had had their disagreements, but if a situation was sufficiently serious he was as loyal as the others. Zoot watched him without comment. Although he said nothing his face showed that he was shocked and hurt.
60 'Pour us another round, Oubaas,' he said slowly and deliberately, turning his back on the activity next door.

They continued drinking, speaking amongst themselves and behaving as if nothing was happening. The level of wine in the can sank lower and lower as the afternoon waned.
65 Pretty-Boy accompanied the lorry on two trips to Schotsche Kloof. It was now almost packed for the last trip. He was tying down some

---

9 **scattered**: lying around   11 **forlorn**: empty and sad   **adjacent**: next (to sth.)
37 **sheepishly**: kleinlaut   44 **hell to pay**: big trouble   53 **drain sth.**: empty sth.
64 **wane**: come to an end

furniture with a thick rope. Moena broke away and hurried down to the Casbah.

'Don't take it too badly,' Mary comforted her. 'We will all have to go in the end. I am really happy for you. At least you're going to Rose Street, where you'll have old friends around you.'

Moena took her farewells of The Butterfly and Miss Sophie but could not contain herself when she kissed her cousin. The two Moenas embraced and spoke softly for the last time.

'You must come and stay with us. We'll have a large spare-room standing empty.'

Mr and Mrs Abrahams were already sitting in the lorry and instructed the driver to sound his hooter for Moena. She stopped at the stoep where The Boys were still sitting. No-one looked up from their drinking. They could forgive her moving but could not forgive her coming between Pretty-Boy and their leader. That was unforgivable.

'Please don't be too hard on him,' she said, indicating Pretty-Boy, who stood lonely and dejected next to the lorry. 'He did it for my sake.'

'Yes, I suppose that's why he did it,' Zoot said without looking at her. 'Have a good time in Rose Street.'

'I'm going to miss you all, especially you, Zoot. Maybe I'll see you when I visit Pretty-Boy.' The hooter sounded impatiently. 'I must go now. Goodbye all of you.'

The lorry drew away and Pretty-Boy watched it disappearing. The Boys picked up the empty can and the glasses and went inside. Pretty-Boy followed and stood forlornly in the door. Zoot stared hostilely at him. Then he looked away.

'After this I need another drink badly. Anything left?'

Oubaas grinned. 'No more,' he said. 'We finished the lot.'

'I have a bottle of something in my room,' Pretty-Boy volunteered. 'I need a drink badly too.'

Zoot stared hard. No-one said anything.

'I have a contact in town who gave me a bottle of the finest whisky. Shall I fetch it?'

Zoot thought about the offer for a long time while Pretty-Boy watched him meekly.

'OK, you can get it,' Zoot said at last.

They drank as if it were old times again.

When Amaai drove up in the Globe Furnishers van he half-expected
what he found. Nevertheless he stared at 205 for a long time. Then he
40 walked around the house. The curtains were all removed and all the
doors locked. He peered inside wherever he could. The Boys came out
onto their stoep and sat watching him. He walked over to them.

'Where did they go?'

'Rose Street, I think,' Zoot said.

45 'So they went there after all. When?'

'They were busy the whole day.'

'Without a word to me.' He said this bitterly.

'You mean you didn't know?'

'I knew they were planning to move but they never said when. I
50 haven't spoken to them for weeks. How did they move?'

'There was a lorry with a driver and his assistant.'

'Any of you help them?'

No-one answered.

'You help them, Pretty-Boy?' There was a mean look in Amaai's eyes.

55 'Nobody here helped,' Zoot said. 'We watched but nobody helped.'

'Not even him?' he asked glaring at Pretty-Boy.

'Not even him,' Zoot said quietly.

Amaai rose and went back to the van. He searched in the boot and
removed a huge, heavy spanner. Then he went to his old house and with
60 terrible and quiet ferocity he started smashing the windows, doors and
even the walls where they gave. The Boys watched without comment.
Amaai worked methodically. There were wet patches on his shirt, and
sweat poured down his face. He breathed heavily but did not alter the
pace of the destruction. At last he was finished. He walked back to his
65 van and replaced the spanner in the boot. Without a word or glance at
The Boys he climbed back into his seat and with a screech of tyres pulled
away. They watched the red tail-light until it disappeared from sight past
Cannon Street.

---

35 **meek**: sanftmütig   41 **peer**: look intensively   59 **spanner**: Schraubenschlüssel
60 **ferocity**: wildness   61 **give**: nachgeben   67 **tail-light**: back light

Dieter

Zoot brought the news to Mary that Katzen had collapsed in his shop with a heart attack and had been rushed by ambulance to Groote Schuur hospital. Apparently he had complained of feeling ill that morning but had refused to accept advice to go home. Then after lunch he had fallen unconscious over his desk. Upon arrival at hospital he had been placed   5
immediately in the Intensive Care Unit. The news had already spread all over the District.

'Nobody seems to know how bad he really is, but it must be very serious if they sent for his son in Jo'burg. He is expected to come by plane this evening.'   10

'Poor Katzen,' Mary said. 'I never thought it was right that he stayed all by himself the way he did and with his heart in that condition. He once told me he lived in a room in a building at the top of Long Street. He also said he cooked, washed and sewed for himself, all in that tiny room.'   15

'What did he do with all his money?' Zoot asked.

'Sent it to his son in Jo'burg, I suppose. I hear he's a big-time lawyer up there.'

'If only we had known how really sick he was, maybe we could have helped him. Maybe we could have paid him some of his rent.'   20

'Speak for yourself. I always paid mine on time,' Mary said.

'So would we if we had had it,' Zoot added petulantly.

'You know, I think it would be nice if we could go and visit him at the hospital. After all he is our friend,' Mary said. 'What time do they have visiting hours?'   25

'About seven, I think.'

'Well, it's too late for this evening, but maybe tomorrow we can go. We can take my Austin.'

'You think it will be all right?' Zoot asked hesitantly.

'Of course.'   30

'Won't there be any problems?'

'Such as what?'

'Look, Mary, we all accept Katzen as our friend, but we must also remember that he is a white man. So he'll be in a white ward. Will we be allowed to go into a white ward?'

'I don't know and I don't care. But I think we should go all the same and work it out once we are there. If our friend is seriously ill, then we should visit him. I don't think we can worry about whether the ward is white or black at a time like this.'

'I was only asking.'

'Well then don't ask questions like that. All they can tell us is that we can't go in. But we'll go all the same and we'll take him some nice flowers and a plate of koeksisters. Think he'll like that?'

'Yes, I think he'll like that.'

The following evening just before seven they parked the car and proceeded through the main entrance to the enquiries counter. Mary was carrying a bunch of carnations and Zoot bore the plate of koeksisters. The receptionist they spoke to looked and sounded efficient.

'We wish to visit a patient. His name is Mr Katzen,' Zoot said timidly.

'White or non-white?' she asked briskly.

'He's a Jew.'

'When was he brought in?'

'Yesterday afternoon, I think.'

She opened the admissions register and ran her finger down a column.

'You know what was wrong with him?'

'He had a heart attack. They say he collapsed in the shop.'

'Cardiac arrest. Katzen, Solomon. Yes, He's in I.C.U., that's the Intensive Care Unit. Let me explain to you how to get there.'

Down rows and rows of polished corridors smelling strongly of disinfectant, they walked, following the directions, till they came to what looked like the unit. After some hesitation, Zoot approached one of the sisters on duty. She was sitting at her desk at the entrance.

'Yes, can I help you?' she said looking up.

22 **petulant**: bockig   35 **white ward**: Station für Weiße   47 **carnation**: Nelke

'We've come to see Mr Katzen.'

'Oh yes, Mr Solomon Katzen. I'm terribly sorry but you won't be able to see him. His condition is very serious.'

'We were afraid of that,' Mary said.

'Will he live?' Zoot asked. 5

'Well, we can always hope. The doctors are doing their very best, but he is very weak. Do you work for him?'

'No, we're just his good friends.'

'Unfortunately only his son is allowed to be inside. Would you like to speak to him?' 10

'Yes, if that's at all possible.'

'All right, have a seat on the beach outside in the corridor while I fetch him. What did you say your names were?'

'I'm Zoot and this is Miss Mary.'

'Well, I won't be a second. Do have a seat in the meantime.' 15

A dapper, well-dressed man in an expensive dark suit came out and looked up and down the corridor. He did not seem to take in the two sitting quietly on the bench. He was about to go back when Zoot stood up.

'You Mr Katzen's son?' he asked. 20

'Yes,' he said, noticing them for the first time. Zoot was still clutching the plate of koeksisters.

'My name is Zoot and this is Miss Mary. We are good friends of your father's.'

He began extending his hand but withdrew when he realised that his 25 greeting was not being reciprocated.

'So then, what can I do for you?' He sounded businesslike.

'We live in your father's houses in Caledon Street.'

'Yes?'

'So we came to see how he is.' 30

'Well, there's really no hope. He was too far gone when he got here. It's just a matter of time.'

'Poor man,' Mary said to herself.

Dieter seemed impatient and ill at ease with them. 'Well, if that's all, then I must go back inside. Thank you all the same for calling.' 35

He was about to leave when Zoot stopped him.

'We would like your father to know how we feel about him. He was always very kind to us. He was a good man. He told us how they treated him in Germany because he was a Jew. We now know how Jews feel.'

40 'Oh yes, he had a hard time, but so did many others.'

'He told us that the Jews suffered then almost the way we are suffering now.'

Dieter made no comment.

'And he told us that it was because of the way he had suffered that he 45 wanted to help us. He said he would never sell his houses to the Group Areas while we lived in them.'

'My father was a sick man for a long time. He was often not responsible for what he said.'

Zoot did not like what he heard.

50 'We came to see him not because of the houses but because he was sick. He is our friend.'

'Well, then, thanks again for coming, but I really must go back now.'

'Will you remember to tell him that we came? The names are Zoot and Miss Mary.'

55 'Yes, all right.'

He smiled slightly as he accepted the gifts, then turned sharply on his heels and went back into the ward.

Mary and Zoot walked back to the car and neither felt like speaking.

60 Two days later the news spread throughout the District that Katzen had died early that morning. When Zoot came to tell Mary she had already heard and was sitting alone crying softly to herself.

'I would never have thought that I would feel so sorry about that old man.'

65 Zoot sat down dejectedly next to her.

'I don't care if we have to leave the houses now. I'm just sorry that he's dead,' she continued.

'I believe the funeral's this afternoon at five o'clock in the Jewish cemetery in Pinelands.'

---

26 **reciprocate sth.**: etwas erwidern   65 **dejected**: sad

'You going?' Mary asked him.

'I thought about it,' Zoot began. 'I gave it a lot of thought this morning, but in the end I decided I wouldn't go. I feel that his son will not be happy with us there.'

'Well, I think we must go all the same even if it's just to show our respect.'

'No, Mary. No matter how good he was, and I admit he was a good friend to us although we never saw it, Katzen is a white man. His son made it clear to me that his father was a white man.'

'But that's not fair,' Mary said reproachfully.

'He didn't say it in so many words, but that is what he meant. He thought we came to the hospital because we were afraid of being put out of the houses.'

'How can you say that, Zoot.'

'It might sound cruel but I'm saying it all the same because that's the way I see it. We will not be welcome at the funeral so I've decided I will not go.'

'You must go for Katzen's sake. Me and The Girls will go.'

'That is your decision. You go for all of us. Go to show all that's left of Buckingham Palace.'

'Zoot, you are making me angry. We've been friends for a long time. We've known Katzen for a long time. The least we can do is to go to his funeral.'

'Me and The Boys will not be there, and that's final. We are tired of being pushed here and being pushed there. If we're not welcome, then we won't go. We are not prepared to be humiliated and to embarrass Mr Dieter. He can have his white funeral to his white self.'

'I don't think he meant it like that. Dieter is an educated man, a lawyer. Educated people don't always show their feelings. But I am not insisting. You can please yourself. If you don't want to go, then you mustn't go. Now you must leave because I'm getting even more upset.'

Mary and The Girls put on their best black dresses and covered their heads with heavy scarves. When they arrived at the Pinelands cemetery the coffin was already in the chapel. The two front rows were occupied by what seemed family and friends of Katzen. There were only eight people, three women in black and five men with yarmulkas perched on

the back of their heads. Mary recognised Dieter immediately, sitting
aloof and reserved in the front row.

   She and The Girls sat in the back row waiting for the service to begin.
Then The Butterfly nudged her gently as Zoot and The Boys filed into
40 the row opposite them. They looked awkward and uncomfortable in
badly pressed clothes but each one of them was wearing an *onder
kuffiyeh* they must have hastily borrowed from Muslim friends in the
District. Mary nodded and smiled at Zoot, who smiled back self-
consciously. Then the Abrahamses arrived. Moena and her mother had
45 their heads covered with lace scarves, and Amaai and his father were
also wearing *onder kuffiyehs*. The entire two back rows of the chapel
were now occupied by Buckingham Palace. Dieter looked around once
only but showed no sign of recognition.

   As the nearest male relative, he rose and stood in front to recite the
50 Kaddish. The sanctification of the Name of God, the affirmation of the
meaningfulness of life and the hope for redemption and ultimate healing
of suffering mankind. Mary looked from Dieter to Amaai, who sat
opposite her. The facial similarity was striking. Both had the same sallow
complexions, the same hair colour and texture, and the same fine facial
55 bone structures. Maybe the Arabs and the Jews were related. Maybe they
were cousins.

   '… glorified and sanctified be God's great name reflected; hallowed
be Thy name throughout the world He has created according to His will.
May his great name be blessed, and the power and the glory, for ever
60 and ever, to all eternity.'

   The pall-bearers took their places and carried the coffin outside for
the burial. Dieter stared straight ahead of him without a glance as they
passed the back rows, As the mourners broke into the sunlight they
passed a group waiting near the open grave. Mary spotted Mr and Mrs

---

25 **humiliate sb.**: jdn. demütigen   37 **aloof**: distanced   39 **nudge sb.**: push sb. with
your elbow   43–44 **self-conscious**: unsure   50 **sanctification**: act of calling sth.
holy   **affirmation**: Bekräftigung   51 **redemption**: Erlösung   53 **facial similarity**:
their faces look similar   **sallow**: unhealthy, yellowish colour   61 **pall-bearer**:
carrier of the coffin   63 **mourner**: person at the funeral

Knight, Faith and Charity amongst them. She smiled her recognition
but Mrs Knight looked away.

Spadefuls of earth rained down heavily on the coffin giving the burial
an air of finality. Zoot stood with Mary and The Girls. The women cried
softly, except for The Butterfly who showed no visible emotion. The   5
group remained standing there until the coffin was completely covered
with earth.

When the burial was over, Mrs Abrahams condoled briefly with
Dieter, who seemed impatient to get away. Finally he left in the company
of the official mourners. The small Caledon Street group remained   10
together, reluctant to break apart. But finally they also had to leave.
Mary and The Girls and Zoot and The Boys went back to Buckingham
Palace, and the rest went to their homes in different places.

The Casbah

It was drizzling heavily one afternoon when a sleek, black Mercedes
15 Benz pulled up outside the Casbah with a squelch of wet tyres. Mr Dieter
Katzen got out carefully to avoid the dirty puddles of rain-water in the
street. He looked far older than his real age and was conservatively
dressed in a black Homburg and an expensive Burberry raincoat. He
was wearing an umbrella which he did not unfurl. He banged impatiently
20 at the door until it was opened by The Butterfly.

'For goodness sake you don't have to bang like that. Most people
inside are still asleep.'

'I would like to come in out of the rain,' he said in a tone that was
more a demand than a request.

25 'Well, then, come in quickly,' she said holding the door wide open,
'but it is still far too early.'

He entered dripping water onto the polished linoleum.

'My name is Katzen, Mr Dieter Katzen.'

'I don't care what the hell your name is. What do you want so early
30 in the afternoon?'

'I own these houses.'

'You do, do you?'

She looked at him more carefully and then recognised him from the
funeral.

35 'I'm the late Mr Katzen's son. These houses have been left to me so
I'm looking around. You don't mind, do you?' he asked sarcastically.

'Well, I suppose you've got a right to do so if it is yours.'

'I hear you people run a somewhat indecent business here.'

'Wait a minute, mister, you'd better tell that to the lady in charge. I
40 don't think she's going to like you. Wait one minute while I fetch Miss
Mary.'

'Yes, I've met her before.'

---

3 **spadefuls of earth**: Spaten voller Erde   8 **condole**: say how sorry one is
14 **sleek**: schnittig   16 **puddle**: little pool of water   18 **Homburg**: type of hat
19 **unfurl sth.**: open sth. (esp. an umbrella)   35 **late**: verstorben

The Butterfly left and Dieter walked around peering into rooms and the kitchen. The Butterfly returned with the information that Mary would be coming in a moment.

'You people seem to have neglected the place.'

'What do you mean?'   5

'I mean you haven't been looking after the house. The walls are damp.'

'So what?'

'It's a bad condition and on top of it the house has an unsavoury reputation.'   10

'Mister, I don't at all like what you're suggesting.'

'I'm not suggesting, I'm saying it. The place is falling apart. I am also not impressed by the use to which it has been put. Fortunately that will end soon.'

Mary came in. She was curious about the visitor and still in dressing-   15
gown and slippers.

'Good afternoon, Mr Katzen?' she said inquiringly.

'Afternoon,' Dieter replied tersely. 'Since we have met before we can dispense with the formalities. My late father has left me all his property. I'm his sole heir. I am at present negotiating with the Department of   20
Community Development for them to purchase these houses.'

'What you are saying is that you are selling them to the Group Areas.'

'Call it what you may. I don't think it will be my responsibility much longer.'   25

'And then we get thrown out. Is that it?'

'That could be it, but that will be their business, not mine. They must decide what to do with you.'

Mary was getting very worked up.

'I wish to remind you that your father promised us he would never   30
put us out.'

'That was my father.'

'And you are your father's son?'

'All I am doing is to negotiate the sale of this property. Once that is through then what they decide to do with it is their affair, not mine.'   35

'But your father promised,' Mary said desperately. 'He was a very sick man, but he promised.'

'I agree with you that he was a very sick man. That is all the more reason why he is not entirely responsible for what he said. I cannot be expected to carry out any promises. I only have your word for it.'

'Are you calling us liars?' The Butterfly asked heatedly.

'Take it as you wish. All I'm trying to say is that I cannot be held responsible for what someone else promised, even if it was my father.'

'You are saying that your father did not know what he was doing?'

'It's very possible.'

'Listen, mister,' The Butterfly said, standing right in front of him. 'I was present in that church vestry when he spoke to us. I admit that he was very sick but he was in full control of himself. He told us how he suffered in Germany and how because of that he wouldn't want to see us suffer also.'

'I'm sure my father meant well, but you should have realised that he was not entirely in control of himself.'

'Maybe he would have been more in control of himself if he had been looked after properly,' The Butterfly flared.

'Just a minute,' Dieter said, now losing his patience.

'I agree with all that Butterfly has said,' Mary added. 'Your father told me himself that he lived alone in a small room at the top of Long Street with no-one to look after him. What did you do about it? I'll tell you. You did sweet blow-all. You sat on your backside in Jo'burg, on your fine, young, white backside, while your father was being neglected down there.'

'He had plenty of his own money. He need not have lived the way he did.'

'He needed more than money. He needed love and understanding. Did you give him any?'

'I see no reason why I should answer your questions. I've now had enough. I cannot allow this conversation to continue. Who do you think you're talking to?'

'To you, Mr Rich White Man. We're talking to you,' The Butterfly said.

---

20 **sole heir**: Alleinerbe   54 **flare**: (here) say sth. in an angry voice   59 **sweet blow-all** (sl): absolutely nothing

'What happens in our family is our business. How my father chose to live was his business.'

'And you were quite contented to know that he was living like that?' The Butterfly asked. 'Tell me, were you ashamed of your father?'

'How dare you suggest that!' 5

'Were you ashamed of him?' the Butterfly insisted.

'I think your behaviour to him was immoral,' Mary added.

'You're a fine one to think that. What about your behaviour? What sort of a house do you run? You pretend to me that you were my father's friends while you abused his kindness by using his premises for your 10 illegal business? Oh, I know you paid the rent on time, but where did you get the money from to pay the rent? And my accountants tell me that your friends next door never paid a cent in rent for all the time they lived here. If that is not immoral, then what is? So don't try to play the grand ladies with me.' 15

'You know,' said The Butterfly, shivering all over with anger, 'you are a disgrace to your father. He was a good and kind man. He told us about his parents in Germany, your grandparents. They were also good and kind people. How can you belong to the same family and still be so mean and cruel and say such unkind things?' 20

All this time Dieter had remained standing. He picked up his umbrella which was leaning against the wall, and his knuckles showed white. Then he turned to leave.

'Thank you for all your uncalled-for advice. The next time you'll hear from me it will be through the lawyers or better still you will hear 25 directly from the Department of Community Development. And, thanks to you, madam,' he turned to The Butterfly, 'you will all soon be without a roof over your heads.'

'Get the hell out of here,' The Butterfly said lunging at him. She was screaming hysterically and Mary had to restrain her. Dieter Katzen left 30 hurriedly and fumbled in the rain to unlock his car door.

Two weeks later registered letters from the Department were delivered to the two households. That evening Zoot and The Boys came over to the Casbah. An air of hopelessness hung over the group. They seemed to be together for mutual comforting, seeking a temporary respite from 35 a situation which was already well beyond them. They sat talking in the growing dark, knowing that there was no possibility of a reprieve.

'You know,' Zoot began, 'my guardian angel always used to tell me how it hated anyone who neglected his father.'

40 The observation raised no immediate response except from Oubaas, who grinned knowingly.

Then Mary said, 'Let us not be as cruel and unfair to that man as he was to us. All he did was to sell these houses.'

'Yes, but he sold it to *them*.'

45 'To whom else could he sell them?'

'He need not have sold them to anyone. He could have kept them as his father had promised. He doesn't need the money. He knew the Department would be only too glad to get rid of us. So what does Mr White Lawyer do? He sells the houses to the Department and then
50 politely washes his hands of the whole affair.'

'Like Pontius Pilate,' Oubaas said nodding wisely.

'That is correct, Oubaas, like Pontius Pilate,' Zoot agreed.

'I still say that all he did was to sell the houses, which he had every right to do. After all they are his houses. He lives far away in Jo'burg, not
55 here in Cape Town. So how do you expect him to look after the houses from so far away?'

'Maybe you're right, but how does all that help us? So he has sold the houses and that gets rid of him. Now we get letters from the Department and that gets rid of us. All right, let's all be fair to him. He didn't
60 personally send the letters, but it's because of him that the letters were sent. Not so?' Zoot asked.

'I'm only saying that we mustn't behave like him.'

Zoot was silent for some time, then said slowly, 'We cannot fight this thing alone. We must join up with others who are already fighting, with
65 those who are losing their houses and are afraid of also losing their manhood. We must join up with all the other so-called *untermenschen*. Only that way we can win. We lost because we tried to fight this thing

22 **knuckle**: Fingerknöchel   30 **restrain sb.**: hold sb. back   31 **fumble**: fummeln
32 **registered letter**: Einschreiben   35 **temporary respite**: vorübergehender
Aufschub   37 **reprieve**: Begnadigung

alone. It's not a Buckingham Palace thing. Not only our houses are being demolished, it is not District Six that is being thrown down, but the whole country. I know what I will do. I know with whom I will work.'

'And what are you going to do, Mary?' Pretty-Boy asked.

She had been staring hard at the table while Zoot was speaking. Now she started slowly without looking up.

'Maybe Zoot is right. Maybe if I had been younger and stronger I would also know what to do. I don't want to leave the District. Believe me, I don't want to leave all you people. I want to fight the way Zoot says we must. I want to remain with you until everything comes crashing down. But this thing is bigger than anything I can cope with.'

'Not if we all stand together,' Zoot said.

'What can eight of us do?'

'We are not eight. We are eight thousand, more than eight million. We are all those who suffer in this sad land.'

'My arms are far too old and weak to fight any more.' Mary did indeed look a tired old woman as she sat staring at the table. 'Everyone around here has given up and is leaving or being forced to leave the District, so we might as well leave also.'

'Not everyone, Mary. We're still here,' Zoot said. 'But if they force us out we'll form another group somewhere else, and if they put us out there, we'll from another group somewhere else. They can't put us out for ever. And one day we'll come back.'

'It's no use. Of the five houses in Buckingham Palace, three are already standing empty. Tomorrow there will be one more. How do you fight these people with your bare hands?'

'You don't give up. You just go on fighting.'

'So what are you planning to do, Mary?' Pretty-Boy asked gently.

'I think it's time I also left. I know it's cowardly but I am tired and want to get away from all this. I want to go as far as possible.'

'As long as you don't forget what they have done,' Zoot insisted.

'Where'll you go, Mary?' Pretty-Boy insisted quietly.

'I am going back to the Boland. I am going to look after my father. He is an old man and needs me. He must not die in a lonely room in Long Street. Maybe you're right, Zoot. Maybe I should stay with you and fight. Maybe what I am doing is wrong. But I promise you that, wherever I am, I will not forget.'

'We're going to miss you,' Zoot said.

'And I'm going to miss you too, because I will not forget.'

40 The Butterfly, who had been listening all the while without speaking, now got to her feet. She seemed to be wrestling with herself and she twisted her mouth nervously as she tried to speak.

'I know that I'm the cause of all this,' she began crying softly. 'If I had not been so rude to that Mr Dieter, he wouldn't have sold our houses.'

45 'You mustn't blame yourself,' Moena said.

'I know it's because of me that you must all go. Mary saw how rude I was to him. I threatened him and made him very angry, so he left and went to sell the houses. He told me it was because of me. Now we've been told to get out.'

50 'It's not because of you. The notices would have come anyway,' Pretty-Boy said.

'Don't be silly and torture yourself,' Moena added.

'I know that I am the one responsible, no matter what you all say. You are being kind and that makes it even worse. You must please excuse 55 me but I can't take it any more.' She left in tears and hurried to her room.

The following morning The Butterfly was gone. There was a note on the kitchen dresser. Mary read it aloud to Moena and Miss Sophie.

'By the time you get this I will be gone, maybe near, maybe far, but 60 gone away. I know it's because of me that all this has happened. Since, as Mary says, everyone is going, maybe it's time I went too. Mary is going back to the Boland and I know that Moena and Miss Sophie have been asked by Mrs Abrahams to come and live with them in Rose Street, so that leaves only me. I don't want to be a burden on anyone. Don't try 65 and find out where I am. Where there's men there's me. I will miss you all, and tell Zoot that I also will not forget.'

The last evening at the Casbah, Mary invited Zoot and The Boys over for farewell drinks. She was leaving in the morning with the transport van which was coming to fetch her furniture. Moena and Miss Sophie had 70 already shifted their belongings to Rose Street. Zoot had removed the

70 **belongings** (pl): all the things they own

red bulb from its socket. An air of depression permeated the almost empty rooms.

They spent the time reminiscing about the past and remembering the characters and the incidents. They spoke softly about Last-Knight and Knight-Before-Last, and Faith, Hope and Charity; about how dangerous it was in Hanover Park and Manenberg; about the Abrahamses 5 and how kind it was of them to take in Moena and Miss Sophie; about the Jungle Boys and their timid sister; about New Year's Day and Kalk Bay; about Father Rowland, who had retired to England; about Mr Theo Plaatjies B.A., who had emigrated with his family to Canada; about Star Bioscope and the National; about Moodley and Baptiste; about Katzen 10 and his son. And always they spoke about District Six.

They drank steadily and as the evening waned they became more sentimental. Finally Zoot got up shakily and said he wanted to propose a toast. He told everyone to stand but asked Mary to remain seated.

'Will you please fill up for the last time. My guardian angel has told 15 me that I must say the last few words in the Casbah. As you know, for years I have had a very talented guardian angel. It used to help me with my poetry when I was young and with my tap-dancing. Then later it used to help me with my speeches. But my guardian angel also speaks about retiring, although as guardian angels go it is still young. I have 20 asked it to help me now especially with the hardest speech I have ever made.

'I want to speak about Mary, a woman who, although she had no children of her own, was nevertheless the mother of the Casbah and of Winsor Park. When I came to Buckingham Palace, it was Mary who 25 gave me my first job as a bouncer and handyman in this house. When I shifted into Winsor Park, it was Mary who helped me. Over the years, when I needed assistance, there was always Mary. When I was depressed, there was always Mary. When I was happy and wanted someone to laugh with, there was always Mary. She says she is leaving us to look 30 after her father, but I know that her heart will always be here. The Casbah will be empty tomorrow but Mary will still be here. Buckingham Palace will be razed next week, but Mary will still be here. And even when District Six is gone, there will still be Marys here. Because they can never destroy our Marys. Mary is District Six. 35

'May your guardian angel remain with you, Mary, wherever you are, and may all your guardian angels remain with all of you wherever you go.'

Mary remained seated while the rest stood and drank to her. Moena
40 Mooies, Miss Sophie and Oubaas were crying softly. Then tears began to course down her cheeks also and without looking up she said fiercely, 'I promise you all, I will never forget.'

The following day the Casbah was empty.

---

1 **socket**: part holding a light bulb   13–14 **propose a toast**: einen Trinkspruch ausbringen   33 **raze sth.**: destroy sth. completely   41 **course down**: kullern

Winsor Park

All the boys at Winsor Park realised that sooner or later the axe would
have to fall. It did so, but sooner than they had expected. The day the
officials from the Department arrived in a government car, Zoot was not
at home. Where he went the boys were unable to say and he never
spoke about it to them. A few days before a white man had been going   5
around in the District asking questions and he also asked about Zoot.

The officials parked their car on the vacant lot next to St Mark's
Church. Both wore what looked like regulation belted khaki raincoats
and had hats deep over their heads. One was tall and the other of
medium height. They got out and started inspecting all the cottages.   10
They had keys to the houses and were unlocking doors. Oubaas and
Surprise came out to see what was happening.

'Why are you people still here?' the tall man asked, walking over
with his companion.

'We live here,' Oubaas replied, giving him a friendly grin.   15

'Well, you don't live here any longer. Do you realise that you are
guilty of trespassing?'

'Nobody told us.'

'Well, I'm telling you now. So you'd better be out by tonight. We're
starting demolition early tomorrow morning.'   20

'At what time?'

'That's none of your business. Just see that you're out by then or we'll
bulldoze you out with all your things as well.'

'We'll tell Zoot when he comes home, that is if he comes home
tonight. But I warn you that he's not going to like it.'   25

'We couldn't care less whether he likes it or not.'

They entered Winsor Park and looked around disapprovingly.

'Get all this rubbish out before we come tomorrow or you'll be in
serious trouble. You understand me?'

Oubaas nodded vigorously. 'I'll give your message to Zoot.'   30

The two finished their cursory inspection, climbed back into their
car and drove off.

The following morning a bulldozer and front-end loader roared up and parked on the vacant field next to the church. Workers from the
35 Department began clearing the grounds and erecting temporary shelters. Officials in helmets and overalls walked around surveying and gauging. In the middle of all these activities Zoot arrived. An official walked over to him.

'You live here?'

40 'Yes,' Zoot began.

'Well, we don't want any trouble. We're starting demolition shortly, so get all your things out as soon as possible. If it's still inside by the time we get to this house, then it will be most unfortunate.'

Soon there was the whine of pneumatic drills and the thud of
45 sledgehammers as blows were rained onto the roof and walls of 209. Clouds of dust swirled around the workmen, who wore handkerchiefs tied around their noses and mouths for protection.

'All right,' Zoot said above the noise, 'we'll let them have their way. There's no use letting them smash our things. So let's move what we can
50 to the field.'

The Boys started lugging and carrying out pieces of furniture, bags of bottles, cooking utensils and rusty tools. The stove and fridge still retained their pink glare of decades before. The battered radiogram received a few extra scratches and dents. For Zoot moving tasted of
55 defeat and he felt humiliated in front of the workers. He worked in bitter silence.

When they had finished, their goods formed an untidy pile next to the church wall. By this time only the broken walls of 209 were left standing. The workmen were now smashing down 207. The Boys
60 squatted down next to their possessions and silently watched the

---

7 **vacant lot**: empty building land   8 **belted**: with a belt around it   17 **trespass**: go onto private land illegally   30 **vigorous**: energetic   31 **cursory**: short and simple   33 **front-end loader**: Schaufelradlader   35 **temporary shelter**: (here) hut for the workers   36 **survey and gauge** [geɪdʒ]: vermessen und maßnehmen   44 **whine**: heulen   **pneumatic drill** [njuːˈmætɪk]: Presslufthammer   45 **sledgehammer**: Vorschlaghammer   46 **swirl**: fly in circles   51 **lug sth.**: pull sth. heavy   55 **defeat**: Niederlage   60 **squat down**: hocken

destruction. Through the clouds of dust whined the tortured screams of the machines and the ear-splitting noise of breaking glass and bursting walls.

'I have found some bottles of wine I thought I had lost,' Pretty-Boy shouted above the noise. 'We might as well finish them now. Surprise, there are cups and glasses in the cardboard box on the fridge.' They huddled together in a small group clutching their drinks as if to help them bear the pain.

By early afternoon three houses were left in ruins, and their walls stuck up starkly through the storm of durst. Zoot walked over to Winsor Park and emerged with a soiled and grimy print of King George VI and his queen.

'I've had this for almost twenty years from the time Katzen first gave it to me. You must give it to your children one day, Pretty-Boy, as a present from us.' He placed it tenderly on the heap.

The pain ran through them again as the Casbah was being smashed down. They stared hypnotised unable to look away. The workers seemed indifferent to the sullen group as they went about their business. The Boys watches hot and red-eyed.

Then finally it was the turn of Winsor Park. They knew it was happening but somehow would not believe their eyes. The pain running through them was now acute. Zoot watched hollow-eyed as the grimy pink walls came crashing down; first the back porch; then the two bedrooms, his and Pretty-Boy's; then the bathroom that had never contained a bath, followed by the kitchen and finally the dining-room where they used to sit and talk for hours. When the dust had settled, the remaining walls stood broken and upright and Winsor Park was now open to the sky.

A whistle blew and all activity for the day came to an end. The machines were switched off and the workmen and officials left for their homes. A silence descended over the ravaged landscape. A chill breeze blew down from Table Mountain. The night-watchman, a huge Xhosa in an old army greatcoat and balaclava, wheeled out his galley from his hut. It was a huge tin drum punctured with holes. He searched around for bits of wood among the debris, carefully placed these inside the tin and then lit a fire. The Boys slowly drifted over towards the warmth till they stood in a circle around it. The night covered everything except the circle of faces lit by the dancing flames. A few sparks spiralled up into the chilly night sky.

40 'Pretty-Boy,' Zoot said quietly, 'when you leave tonight you must go to Rose Street and tell Amaai to bring his van here to fetch what's left. It is a present from us for you and Moena. You might need it one day. What you don't want you can just give away.'

'Thank you, Zoot,' Pretty-Boy said.

45 'I suppose you will live in Bokaap.'

'Yes, or somewhere near there. We want to be near the old people.'

'I know she will make you happy,' Zoot said.

'I also know.'

'And what about the two of you, my friends?'

50 'I don't know yet,' Oubaas began, 'but wherever we go, Surprise and me will go together. Tonight we will sleep under one of those trucks near the station. Tomorrow, who knows where.'

'I'm going to miss you all,' Zoot said.

'And we're going to miss you, Zoot,' Pretty-Boy replied. 'Where are
55 you going to and what are you going to do? You've asked us about ourselves, but told us nothing about your plans.'

The fire in the galley was now burning low and the night getting more chilly. The group moved closer, seeking more than warmth.

'I suppose my guardian angel will still be looking after me even after
60 we all break apart. I know it will not desert me now. This is not the end. It is only the beginning. The greedy people who have taken away our homes will soon have to answer to us. They thought that they had reduced us to **untermenschen** but they lied. We are living proof that they lied. We must always tell our story to our children and to our children's
65 children. They must know. If you have children one day, Pretty-Boy, Moena and you, you must tell them.'

Pretty-Boy nodded intensely.

---

10 **stark**: scharf umrissen   11 **grimy** ['graɪmi]: dirty   18 **sullen**: in a bad mood
31 **ravaged**: destroyed; violated   32 **Xhosa** ['kɔːsə]: Black South African from the
Eastern Cape Province   33 **galley**: (here) oven   60 **desert sb.** [- '-]: leave sb.

'The children must be reminded of the evils that greed and arrogance can cause. We must tell about the District and the thousands of other districts they have broken up because they wanted even more than they already had. We knew that District Six was dirty and rotten. Their newspapers told us so often enough. But what they didn't say was that it was also warm and friendly. That it contained humans. That it was never a place – that it was a people. We must tell how they split us apart and scattered us in many directions like the sparks from this fire. They are trying to destroy our present but they will have to deal with our future. We must never forget.

'Pretty-Boy, you want to know where I'll be. I don't know. But I know where I'm going to and I know what I must do. I promise you that our children and the children of those who are doing this to us will join together and they will see that this will never happen again.'

He paused, emotionally drained. Pretty-Boy took him quietly by the hand in a farewell gesture and then turned towards Tennant Street to go to the Bokaap. Oubaas grinned and mumbled something. Then he and Surprise walked down Severn Steps to the station. None of the three looked back. The watchman saluted Zoot in Xhosa, and went into his hut, shutting the door behind him.

The flame in the galley was very low and licked weakly over the glowing bits of wood. For some time Zoot stood deep in thought staring at it, then he pulled himself together and began to walk down Caledon Street. He also did not look back. The flame flickered for some time determined to stay alive.

7 **split people apart**: divide people

Additional Texts

1
The Group Area Acts

This text was written in the 1960s, as the Group Areas Act was being put into effect. It describes the intention of the Act and its consequences.

The Group Areas Act provided for the establishment of racial ghettoes in which ownership and occupation of land would be restricted to a specified population group. This immensely complicated Act, which cuts across all property rights, has been amended on innumerable
5 occasions and is still in the process of enforcement, with many areas of the country not yet demarcated for the ownership or occupation of any group. Although in the 1962 session of Parliament the Minister of the Interior refused to supply any figures, trends so far indicate that the vast bulk of the country will be reserved for White ownership and occupation.
10 To achieve the racial separation which is contemplated by this Act, hundreds of thousands of people will have to give up their homes and move to other areas; and as might have been expected, the majority of sacrifices will be made by non-Whites.
The general purpose of the removals is to exclude non-Whites from
15 the central areas of all towns and cities, in some of which they have lived for centuries, and to resettle them in newly developed, totally segregated areas on the outskirts. In many of these new areas the inhabitants find that their standard of housing may in some cases have improved, but that they are generally now faced with a total lack of amenities, plus a
20 huge increase in the cost of transport and sometimes even in rents. The following are brief details of the way in which the peoples of the main centres have been affected.
Cape Town and adjoining areas: The total numbers of people affected by Group Areas proclamations up to March 1961 were: White, 7,731;
25 Coloured, 94,148; and Asian 4,658. Subsequently, in terms of Proclamation 43 of 11 February 1966, the most controversial area of the

city – and, despite its poverty and squalor, one of the most cohesive and human – District 6, was set aside for White ownership and occupation. According to figures given by the Minister of Housing in June 1964, there were at that time about 800 Whites, 61,000 Coloured people and 30 Malays, and 600 Indians in the area. The estimated market values of properties there were 17 million Rand for White properties, 6 million Rand for Coloured, 5 million Rand for Indian, and 7 million Rand for municipal and state. The Minister said in the Assembly that about 5,700 families would be involved in the removal; but the likelihood is that, at 35 the end of the ten years which he indicated as necessary to complete the operation, there will not be a single non-White left residing in the area. [...]

There have already been several cases of suicide by non-Whites whose homes and savings have been threatened by the application of 40 the Act. The writer Alan Paton has described the Group Areas Act as the greatest sin which the White people have committed. In a number of areas, leaders of the Indian community have refused to obey removal orders served on them under the Group Areas Act; the former chairman of the Transvaal Indian Congress, sixty-nine-year-old Mr Nana Sita, 45 completed in December 1967 his third jail sentence for refusing to leave the Pretoria home in which he had lived for thirty-seven years.

(From: Brian Bunting, The Rise of the South African Reich, *Harmondsworth: Penguin 1964)*

2 **restricted to**: limited to   3 **specified**: stated in a law, etc.   4 **amend sth.**: change sth. slightly   **innumerable**: very many   6 **demarcated**: marked out   7 **session**: Sitzung   9 **bulk**: majority   10 **contemplate sth.**: etwas in Erwägung ziehen 17 **outskirts**: area outside a city   19 **amenity**: sth. that makes life comfortable and easy   23 **adjoining**: neighbouring, surrounding   24 **proclamation**: Erlass 27 **squalor**: dirty and unpleasant living conditions   **cohesive**: forming a united whole   40 **savings** (pl): Sparnisse   **application**: act of putting sth. into force/effect 44 **serve sth.**: etwas zustellen

2
A Brief Account of District Six

District Six is very close to the centre of the city of Cape Town (five minutes' walk from the City Hall), on the slope of Devil's Peak and Table Mountain running down to the Castle. In the first half of the 19th century it was the major residential area for all those who worked in the
5 city. It was known as Kanaladorp, either from the Malay word *kanala* meaning to help one another, or because it lay to the east of the canal that ran from the Gardens to the Castle. In 1867 Cape Town was divided into six municipal districts, and Kanaladorp became District Six.

By 1900 many of the wealthier merchants had moved out of District
10 Six. With the arrival of railways and tramways they established predominantly white suburbs such as Gardens, Green Point and Sea Point, and the southern suburbs. So District Six increasingly became a working-class area, with many people depen dent on seasonal employment at the docks or in the areas such as fishing, the railways
15 and the building trade. While some white people chose to move out, black African people were moved out of District Six in early attempts at segregation, for example to Ndabeni in 1901.

The population of District Six came from all over the world. The largest number were people whom the Cape Town government referred
20 to as 'Malay', or 'Mixed', or 'Coloured', people who were the descendants of slaves, Khoi, African and the white colonists originally from Europe. Jewish people from Russia, Indians, Chinese, British, Australians were all to be found in District Six.

One historian says:

25 District Six at the turn of the century may have been poor, but it was undoubtedly a vibrant place. It was, arguably, one of the most cosmopolitan areas in the Cape, if not the whole of sub-Saharan Africa. Yet there were no examples of wide-scale racial or ethnic antagonisms.

30 *(Vivian Bickford-Smith, 'Origins and Early History of District Six'. In: Crain Soudien, Shamil Jappie (eds), The Struggle for District Six · Past and Present. Cape Town: Buchu Books, 1990, p. 43)*

Another historian says of District Six in the 1920s and 1930s:

What set District Six apart from the rest of civil society in Cape
Town … was its cosmopolitanism. A child growing up there
might be the progeny of a West Indian seaman and a migrant
Coloured woman from rural Southwestern Cape. Its parents   5
might be a Coloured woman raised in Harfield Village, Claremont,
and a paid-off Scots Fusilier who had settled in Cape Town after
the South African War. It might be borne by a female migrant
from St Helena married to a Lithuanian cabinet-maker. Or its
father might be a Tamil Indian migrant from Natal, with a family   10
history of indentured plantation labour, and its mother a Muslim
woman from a Kalk Bay family with an unmistakably Portuguese
surname.

(Bill Nason, 'Oral History and the Reconstruction of "District Six"'. As above,
pp. 63–64)   15

Over the years the municipal authorities shamefully neglected District
Six and its people: 'Although the Council provided few amenities,
District Six teemed with pubs and canteens, with indoor games,
gambling dens and brothels. And yet the District had an extremely low
rate of violent crime' (Bickford-Smith, p. 43).   20
    When the National Party came to power in 1948 and started to
entrench its apartheid policy, it decided it could use the pretext of slum
clearance to move out many thousands of people from District Six. Its
real reason became blatantly obvious when in 1966 District Six was
proclaimed a white area under the Group Areas Act. Over the next 18   25
years some 60,000 people were forced to move, most of them out to the
Cape Flats. All the houses and buildings of District Six were bulldozed
out of existence. Only the few mosques and churches remained standing,
defiant.
    For some years no one would buy land in the desolate District Six. 30
With what seemed a callous disregard for people's feelings, the
government started to build a technical college, then for white students
only, and some flats for police and military staff. While the technikon is
now open to all, it completely surrounds the small stone St Mark's

35 Church, the Klipkerkie, just next door to where 'Buckingham Palace' once stood.

(From: Robin Malan, Buckingham Palace, *Cape Town: David Philip Publishers, 1996)*

4 **residential area**: area of a town where people live and there is little industry
8 **municipal district**: administrative part of a town 13–14 **seasonal employment**: Saisonarbeit 20 **descendant**: Nachkomme 26 **vibrant** ['vaɪbrənt]: lively
29 **antagonism**: hostility 36 **progeny** ['prɒdʒəni]: Nachkommenschaft
39 **paid-off**: ausgedient **fusilier** [ˌfjuːzə'lɪə] (old-use): soldier 43 **indentured**: forced to work for an employer for a period of time 49 **amenities** [ə'miːnətiːz]: Annehmlichkeiten 50 **teem with**: be full of 54 **entrench sth.**: establish sth.
56 **blatant** ['bleɪtnt]: direct, open 61 **defiant** [də'faɪənt]: trotzend 63 **callous**: heartless

3
Remember

REMEMBER DIMBAZA.
REMEMBER BOTSHABELO/ONVERWACHT,
SOUTH END, EAST BANK,
SOPHIATOWN, MAKULEKE, CATO MANOR.
REMEMBER DISTRICT SIX.   5
REMEMBER THE RACISM
WHICH TOOK AWAY OUR HOMES
AND OUR LIVELIHOOD
AND WHICH SOUGHT
TO STEAL AWAY OUR HUMANITY.   10
REMEMBER ALSO OUR WILL TO LIVE,
TO HOLD FAST TO THAT
WHICH MARKS US AS HUMAN BEINGS:
OUR GENEROSITY, OUR LOVE OF JUSTICE
AND OUR CARE FOR EACH OTHER.   15
REMEMBER TRAMWAY ROAD,
MODDERDAM, SIMONSTOWN.

IN REMEMBERING WE DO NOT WANT
TO RECREATE DISTRICT SIX
BUT TO WORK WITH ITS MEMORY: 20
OF HURTS INFLICTED AND RECEIVED,
OF LOSS, ACHIEVEMENTS AND OF SHAMES.
WE WISH TO REMEMBER
SO THAT WE CAN ALL,
TOGETHER AND BY OURSELVES,   25
REBUILD A CITY
WHICH BELONGS TO ALL OF US,
IN WHICH ALL OF US CAN LIVE,
NOT AS RACES BUT AS PEOPLE.

8 **livelihood** ['laɪvlihʊd]: source of income   12 **hold fast to sth.**: hold on to sth.
with strength   14 **generosity**: kindness, goodness   21 **hurt** (n): wound   **inflict**
sth.: etwas zufügen   22 **achievement**: Errungenschaft

4

An Interview with Joe Schaffers

The following interview was conducted with Joe Schaffers, an ex-resident of District Six, in January 2006.

What are your personal reminiscences of District Six when it was still in existence?

A place of warmth and love, of caring for each other and trying to understand and appreciate each other. Worldly possessions did not
5 matter, there were rich and poor people (of which poor people formed a major part), who shared their day to day existence. What I also remember quite vividly are the beautiful buildings we had in District Six. Some dilapidated, but architecturally works of art.

What was it in the Group Areas Act of 1950 that made the then
10 **government remove 60,000 people and flatten their houses by bulldozers?**

The destruction of District Six was politically motivated. In declaring the area as white, except for the area known as the Bo Kap (the Malay quarter) the whole of the city was now officially 'white.' One finds that
15 only areas of prime property importance in the country were declared as 'white.' District Six was one of those prime property areas.

What were the experiences and feelings of the people resettled to the area of Cape Flats?

The feeling of the vast majority of people was one of hopelessness,
20 helplessness and dehumanised people.

To what extent do the experiences of the ex-residents help to understand the work of the apartheid system?

Being in the museum as an ex-resident I try and give visitors and the youth of today an insight into the mentality of the Apartheid oppressors.

25 **I take it that the people who were forced to leave District Six were of different races, religions and cultures. Who were they?**

You are correct. However, whites were allowed to stay in District Six. All people of colour were required to move. Different races of colour were placed in 'townships' set out for them. The so-called Indian community
30 was placed in Rylands and Cravenbay Estates. The black folk were sent to

areas such as Langa, Gugulethu & Khayelitsha and your so-called coloured folk in areas like Manberg, Bonteheuwel, Heideveld, Retreat, Steenberg, Lavender Hill, Mitchell's Plein to as far as Atlantis on the west coast.

The District Six Museum has deeply impressed me because it is not only a goldmine of information but a place that instils into its visitors 35 *curiosity and a sensitivity for the feelings of the people resettled. How did this museum come into existence?*

District Six Museum came into existence because of a group of activists coming out of the 'Hands Off District Six' campaign (H.O.D.) decided they needed a place of memory. After sourcing other venues it was 40 decided that the Methodist church (which also has a history attached to it) was the most appropriate place. The first exhibition was the 'Streets Exhibition,' which opened on December 10th, 1994 and was supposed to be for only two weeks. But eleven years later, we are still here.

What is currently being done or will be done in the near future to 45 *restore what used to be District Six? Are some of the people who used to live there allowed to return? Are the people who are still alive willing to go back?*

Under the Land Restitution Act people have been able to apply for restitution, the cut-off date being December 31st, 1998. Twenty-four of 50 the most senior people have already moved into District Six, and it is hoped that around another 4,000 homes will be built.

Could you put in a nutshell what District Six meant to you personally in the old days and what it means to you today?

In the old days as I discussed earlier, District Six was a home with family 55 and friends and everything that was familiar to you. Today, it's a space for memories with little to entice me back to it.

Who gave the name Buckingham Palace to the row of houses in District Six?

The name 'Buckingham Palace' was a tongue-in-cheek name given by 60 locals to this dilapidated building in Caledon Street.

---

1 **reminiscence**: memory   7 **vivid**: lively   8 **dilapidated**: run-down, in a bad state of repair   15 **prime**: best, most important   35 **instil sth. into sb.**: make sb. feel or think about sth.   40 **source sth.**: look for sth.   **venue**: place   50 **restitution**: Wiederherstellung   **cut-off date**: deadline   53 **in a nutshell**: briefly   57 **entice sb.**: jdn. locken   60 **tongue-in-cheek**: meant as a joke

The Author

Richard Rive [ri:v] was born in 1930 in District Six, the youngest of six children. He knew almost nothing about his father, who died soon after his birth. He went to St Mark's Primary School and Trafalgar High School, both in District Six, and then to the Hewat College of Education in Athlone, where he qualified as a teacher. He then studied at the University of Cape Town, Columbia University (New York) and Oxford University. For many years he was Head of the English Department at Hewat College, and was athletics coach at a Cape Town high school. He began writing short stories in the early 1960s, but as publishers were not interested in works by non-whites, his first collection of short stories, *African Songs,* was published in East Berlin in 1963. His first novel *Emergency* was published in 1964. His second and best-known work, *Buckingham Palace, District Six,* was published in 1986. Despite being classified as a Coloured, he always believed in non-racialism, and he refused to join any political organization. He was murdered in his home in Princess Vlei, Cape Town, in 1989.